policy analysis and education series

DALE MANN, GENERAL EDITOR

EDUCATION, SOCIAL SCIENCE, and the JUDICIAL PROCESS

Edited by
Ray C. Rist
Ronald J. Anson

TEACHERS COLLEGE PRESS
Teachers College, Columbia University
New York and London

CARNEGIE LIBRARY
LIVINGSTONE COLLEGE
SALISBURY, N. C. 28144

Introductory matter copyright © 1977 by Teachers College, Columbia University

Library of Congress Cataloging in Publication Data
Main entry under title:

Education, social science, and the judicial process.

  (Policy analysis and education series)
  Includes bibliographical references.
  1. Discrimination in education—Law and legislation—
United States—Addresses, essays, lectures.　2. Judicial
process—United States—Addresses, essays, lectures.
3. Social indicators—United States—Addresses, essays,
lectures.　I. Rist, Ray C.　II. Anson, Ronald J.
III. Series.
KF4155.A2E35　　　344′.73′0798　　　77-962
ISBN 0-8077-2532-3

Manufactured in the United States of America

Designed by Angela Foote

344.73
R 597

To Harold "Bud" Hodgkinson—

*American education will reap for years
the benefits of his vision and wisdom,
his integrity and leadership.*

105731

On the Shaping of Educational Policy: The Transition From Administrative/Political to Judicial Decision-Making

Ronald J. Anson
Ray C. Rist

There is a growing awareness that the judicial system in the United States is assuming a new role vis-à-vis the adjudication of political and ethical issues not easily resolved elsewhere. This new role has led to the charge by some that the courts have become more "activist" and thus have strayed from their more proper domain of strict constitutional matters. Alternatively, those who support this expansion of judicial influence argue that it is precisely because of a recognition of the constitutional implications in many of our present problems that judicial intervention is imperative. But aside from the debate over whether the courts are or are not correct in assuming their new role, the reality is that they *are* deeply involved and give every indication of remaining so.

One result of this transition is that the courts are now being called upon to decide matters previously thought to be the responsibility of administrators and public officials. This is especially true vis-à-vis public education. There are few other sectors of our society where the most basic decisions are now either subject to or directed by the courts. Recent cases in the medical profession suggest, however, that other areas of American society are also coming increasingly under the aegis of the courts.

That the locus of decision-making responsibility for the most basic policies and directives of a variety of institutions has shifted can be interpreted as a failure of the traditional centers of decision-making. The failure is essentially one of not being able to achieve a political or ethical consensus about the most appropriate course to follow. The consequence is then that, if the issue is pressing and the impasse must be overcome, there is a need for a final decision-making authority. But a contrary and perhaps more realistic assessment is that the attribution of failure to one group or another is irrelevant. In what is now a highly pluralistic and diverse society, fractured into a variety of nonaligned interest groups, it is a political or administrative impossibility to achieve sufficient consensus on many basic ethical issues. Thus, whether one speaks of abortion, school desegregation, environmental quality, capital punishment, or the limits of individual liberty, the building of a consensus to guide public policy is tenuous at best. And while the political vacuum remains, decisions must be made. So enter the courts.

Further analysis along these lines also suggests that it is increasingly unrealistic to expect public forums or administrators/generalists to have to make final decisions on the basis of knowledge outside their domains. Add to this the fact that these decisions, involving the analysis of complex data sets and factors of multiple causality, are at the same time ethical in their implications for the society. Few, if any, administrators or public officials would necessarily want to have the sole responsibility of making such decisions. To be held liable on either political or legal grounds for a decision on which it is impossible to please everyone (or even almost everyone) is not desirable. The courts are thus setting where final liability can rest and where the adjudication of complex social issues can be accomplished, at least insofar as giving guidance to the actions of responsible officials is concerned.

The courts have increasingly become the setting where we seek to resolve what are otherwise unresolvable public issues. Indeed, the range of such issues is rather astounding. The courts are now providing guidance on when a hospital may or may not turn off a respirator and pronounce a person legally "dead," when an oil pipeline may or may not be built, when as SST may or may not use a particular airport, when publicly supported housing may or may not be built, when an I.Q. test may or may not be used to evaluate a child, etc.

The shift in the laws of decision-making has at least three important implications for how social issues are being adjudicated within the legal arena. First, the courts are having to deal with new forms of information and new methods of analysis for understanding causality. The courts have traditionally been able to reduce complex issues to fit within the language and mode of analysis specific to the legal profession (with the possible exception of psychiatric analysis). This is changing rapidly as social scientists, environmental scientists, medical researchers, and others are introducing data and analyses from within their own disciplinary frameworks and their own modes of analysis. There is, of course, some effort at translation, but much is frequently lost in the process—not all other analytical frameworks are reduceable to the legal framework.

Second (derived from the first implication), new sets of actors are on the stage. Expert testimony to rebut expert testimony, research evidence presented by researchers and not by lawyers, and new groups of defendants/plaintiffs on an increasingly diverse set of issues find their way onto court dockets. Again with specific attention to education, a host of issues have brought teachers, principals, administrators, parents, researchers, property owners, students, juvenile authorities, social workers, and public officials into court. This has not been the traditional setting in which these individuals have been held accountable.

Third and finally, with the movement into the courts and the final authority that rests there, the recourse of the losers in the litigation has been drastically reduced compared to that available through traditional political or administrative channels. Not only are the inputs to decision-making decidedly changed, but so are the legitimate reactions to decisions. In a very real way, highly political issues are rendered apolitical by moving them into the courts, but this is the price paid for finding no other acceptable avenue of resolution.

This movement into the courts of the decision-making authority vis-à-vis broad areas of educational policy has had considerable impact upon all spheres of education—from the daily classroom procedures of teachers through the exercise of authority by principals and administrators to fiscal decisions made by school boards and voters. Matters of school finance, student codes of conduct, disciplinary procedures, school desegregation, student evaluation mechanisms, education for children with special needs, school construction sites, and school district boundaries are but a few of the areas in which the courts have set guidelines and established precedents. The traditional centers of decision-making are finding themselves increasingly in the role of expediting and implementing court rulings.

It would be moving too far afield to pursue further the comparisons and contrasts in decision-making styles between traditional centers of decision-making and the courts. Rather, the more specific task of this analysis is to sketch broadly the manner in which information is gathered, interpreted, and summarized in these respective spheres of decision-making. It is in this way that we have a basis for ascertaining the distinctive contributions of the social sciences to the processes. What follows then is an assessment of the manner in which traditional centers collect and utilize data, and the socio-political context in which decisions are finally made. This is contrasted with the manner in which the courts are able to use information, in what forms such information is admissible, and its relative efficacy in assisting the adjudication process.

Informational Needs in Administrative/Political Decision-Making

Policy-making within the framework of administrative/political processes necessitates that information be gathered to represent widely different views of the issue at hand. Because reality is "socially constructed," it is an imperative that there be this multiplicity of views, for any one view is at best only a partial picture, frequently colored by the source and the expected use of the information. It is in the weighing and shaping of many such assessments that the decision-maker fashions an answer to the problem. The answer is one that should respond not only to the content of the problem, but as well to the interested parties and groups who have a vested interest in the manner in which the problem is approached. The informational needs of policy-makers exist in the context of having to fashion a response where substantive input is but one facet to be considered.

The need to formulate a policy is often thrust upon the policy-maker by an interested party who wishes to have a particular situation or procedure clarified or established. It is in the nature of bureaucratic existence that policy-makers do not spend all their time seeking out new areas in which to make policy. If one sees the policy process as entailing costs as well as benefits, it is poor strategy to continually risk the accumulation of costs beyond those absolutely inevitable.

When pressures for a decision do mount, the policy-maker confronts a situation of multiple constituents, each seeking the decision most favorable to their own view. If the issue is sufficiently developed, each of the parties may present to the policy-maker information and data analyses that they find beneficial to their respective positions. It is here that the political dimension to social "facts" becomes so evident. The greater the number of constituents involved, the more complex the decision-making process becomes: not only does the absolute amount of information input grow, but so also do the variations in interpreting the situation.

One critical dimension of the decision-making process, from the decision-maker's perspective, is the ability to assess the relative outcomes of various options. Particularly important is the need to have some estimation of the role relations among the various interested parties that will result from resolving the issue. The ordering of the social system in which the decision-making process occurs must function at some minimal level of stability; otherwise the entire enterprise of policy-making is not possible. Thus the policy-maker is involved in a continual effort to balance the roles and needs of various constituents as well as to respond to problems as they arise. The goal is to develop responses that in some manner address the problem without too badly upsetting other social arrangements—witness the school superintendent and school desegregation efforts.

Because the policy-making process necessitates present decisions to affect future events, and because social situations change in their dimensions and our understandings of them, there must be continuous feedback of information to the policy-maker. Thus the policy-maker has reasonable grounds upon which to seek alterations during the implementation of a decision. In contrast to the view that information input is a "once and for all" event, we can posit that information needs are continuous throughout the policy-making process—from the formulation of the problem, to the weighing of various options, to the decision on a particular course of action, to the implementation stage, when the policy-maker needs to assess just how successful a decision was in responding to the issue, to the necessity of reformulation when the inevitable gap between theory and practice is exposed.

Another aspect of the information needs of the decision-maker is what may be called "degrees of certainty." What is implied here is that, with any factual presentation, there should be included some assessment of just how strong the likelihood of the option's being effective is. If a decision-maker knows, for example, that a very narrowly defined option is likely to have high impact upon a small population, and that a broadly based option is less certain to be effective, but would impact many more persons if it did work, he or she thus has key information to discriminate between options. It is here that such factors as political risk taking, system stability, and centrality of the issue supersede the information base in making the final decision.

Were the process described above followed in every instance of policy-making, it is obvious that there would be a never-ending need for both policy-makers and information processers. But reality intrudes through the absolute limits imposed by time, resources, and talent. What more realistically occurs is that less important issues are dealt with in a less intensive and exhaustive manner, and resources are allocated toward those efforts more critical to the functioning of the organization, the careers of the individuals involved, and the resolution of immediate, conflict-laden situations. Although this setting of priorities is seldom mentioned in the policy-studies literature, we call attention to it here because it is a key element of the entire process. When priorities are set and the various types of resources allocated, activities are set in motion that begin to generate their own consequences. The result is increasing difficulty in rearranging the original priority listing.

If one were to distill from this foregoing analysis a "pure" model of the informational needs and the role of systematic research in the policy-making process, it would appear very close to that offered by Costner, who is quoted below to summarize our understanding of information needs within the administrative/political decision-making context.

> Policy research, as commonly conceived, entails providing information services for decision makers—usually visualized as a group of legislators or government administrators. The decision makers then take these research findings into account in coming to a decision on the issues pending before them. The simpler and more naive conception of policy research suggests that the decision makers should be persuaded by the cogency of the findings and make their decisions accordingly. A more complex conception assumes the decision makers and their reactions are more varied. Those who favor the decision implied or supported by the policy researcher's conclusions hail the results as definitive and use the information provided in support of their position. Those who were initially undecided are convinced by the policy researcher's conclusions and join with those initially favorable. Finally, those who find the policy researcher's conclusions contrary to the stand they favor denounce the conclusions as biased and unsound, and seek alternative information—and maybe an alternative policy researcher—to provide support for their own views. Hence, as this conception has it, policy researchers provide ammunition for debate among decision makers even if the research conclusions do not determine the decision by the sheer wieght of the evidence.[1]

Information Needs in Judicial Decision-Making

Given the scenario described above by which administrative/political policy-making takes place, the incursion of the courts into the policy-making domain seems ill suited at best. Court cases traditionally have concerned themselves with defining rights and duties of parties to an action; establishing a breach of duty, usually with some allocation of fault; discovering an injury to the interest of another party; and fashioning a remedy to right the wrong. The guidelines by which a party can present its case are established rules of law. All information must fall within the narrow confines of relevant evidence pertaining to a specific point of law contained in the party's legal case. The inevitable result of such precise directives is that much information relevant in one way or another to the case must be excluded. The loss of an expanded information base is the sacrifice paid for universalistic criteria about the submission of evidence.

Furthermore, the legal approach to conflict resolution opperates in a rather specialized context. Litigation arises from a party's perception that he or she has been harmed. Seldom are anticipated wrongs the basis for court action, however. The role of the courts is to provide a forum for the hearing of evidence related to a specific activity and to reach some sort of rectification so as to return the involved parites, where possible, to the *status quo ante.* The remedies available to the court are also circumscribed. They must be appropriate to the particular case and the parties involved, as well as congruent with previous decisions and remedies in the same general area. The net effect of such constraints is to limit the impact of any single legal decision. Each decision then becomes an incremental addition to a chain of decisions that are analogous to the present one and that have been decided in much the same way. This legal doctrine, *stare decisis,* undergirds legal thinking and thus provides both continuity and universality to the methods of judicial decision-making.

In making determinations about the rights and duties of the parties to a suit, the court receives information about the status and circumstances of the parties and events under scrutiny. This information is generally descriptive (psychiatric testimony is an exception), and is used in determining what the legal relation is among the contending parties and what will be the legal significance of their acts. Once such information has been presented and is admissible to the court, the findings must flow from the presented information. There is an array of rules governing court procedures that prohibits the introduction of much evidence that would be used by a decision-maker functioning within an administrative/political context. Hearsay, opinions not supported by direct evidence, and political considerations, for example, are all excluded as potentially biased to the adjudication process. Whether it be by a judge or a jury, determination of the suit is to be based soley on presented evidence.

If it is established that a legal relation does exist between the parties, the court then examines the activity involved to determine if a right was violated or a duty breached. This is usually associated with the attaching of fault to one of the parties. Again, the information provided must be directed at the narrow question of the activity in question. Collateral information is allowed in certain rigidly prescribed circumstances, but always under rules limiting rather than expanding the court's ability to probe the full range of possible variables in relation to the activity. The legal basis upon which breach of duty is established is well codified through an elaborate set of rules of law. If certain preconditions can be established according to these rules, then the determination of a breach is unavoidable. Any other information is extraneous.

If the task of the court is to ascertain injury as opposed to breach, then the court does have more flexibility in allowing evidence and judging the merits of that information. The range of possible injuries is broad and less restricted by prior legal codes than are other elements of a legal suit.

Injury or loss due to the actions of one of the parties to a suit is almost without exception a factual determination, dependent upon the establishing of causal relations between the actions of one party and the loss of another.

(Of necessity, it must also be shown that in fact a loss did occur.) In the effort to show loss or injury, the courts will allow testimony from a variety of experts, eyewitnesses, and participants to build as full a picture of the relation between the parties as is possible. This is necessary because the codifications of law simply cannot anticipate all possible injuries or all possible manifestations of loss. Such information is critical to the determination of whether causality exists. It is in this instance that the broad scope of information needs come closest to those of the administrative/political decision-maker. But even here, there are a considerable number of restrictions inherent in legal procedure that give the court a more narrow view of the activity in question. It is in the ascertaining of loss that social science evidence may be important—witness the economic analyses of disparities in school finance measures, the maintenance of *de jure* school segregation, and the role of student evaluations in affecting educational opportunities.

If the court finds compelling evidence of injury or loss, the final stage of litigation is to fashion a remedy. The purpose of a remedy is to put the parties in as close proximity as possible to the position they would occupy had there been no injury and no loss. Frequently, this is done through the awarding of damages to the injured party. The discretion of the courts is rather broad in attempting to fashion the remedy. Not being tightly bound by predetermined regulations allows for some degree of latitude and creativity on the part of the court in responding to the causal relation set forth in the litigation. We need only to survey the variations in school desegregation remedies to have a sense of the divergent approaches used by different judges.

Although this discussion gives some sense of our own belief that there is movement within the legal profession and within judicial procedure to broaden the inquiry upon which determinations are based, the standards are more often than not still quite explicit and circumscribed. The courtroom remains far from a market place of open and unfettered discourse—as in fact is proper. But with the changes in the judicial scope of inquiry and the domains over which judicial authority has now spread, rigid adherence to the most traditional and narrowly defined basis for legal procedure seems both antiquated and counterproductive. The following matters appear to need reexamination: (1) The inability of third parties or other interested groups to be incorporated in the inquiry except in extreme circumstances; (2) the narrow interpretation of past acts with little or no consideration given to side or ripple effects; (3) the lack of means to modify judicial remedies once set in motion; and (4) the tendency on the part of the courts to terminate involvement once the remedy decree is issued. In each of these areas, what appears necessary is to develop the means by which to supply information to the courts commensurate with their broadened responsibilities.

Education, Social Science, and the Judicial Process

Given the rather limited domain of action available to the courts, it would seem unlikely that they represent a serious infringement upon the traditional policy-making prerogatives of administrative/political officials. Nevertheless, the courts have so moved and are now creating policies at all levels of the society. Perhaps the most dramatic area where this is happening is in what is termed "public law litigation." Whether this movement is due to a belief in more activism by the judges or to the gradual accumulation of changes in the rules of the courts, it is difficult to say. But certainly the changes in the rules on standing to sue, in the scope of equitable relief in class action suits, and in the groups in the society now turning to the courts for assistance have exposed the courts to a far broader range of social issues than previously. In all this expansion, the need of the courts for greater and different kinds of information than had heretofore been part of legal proceedings has been apparent. The continual expansion of the net by which the courts seek to collect evidence necessary to determine social facts has meant the task of "fact finding" becomes more and more central to the adjudicative process.

The contrast between the "fact finding" mechanisms available to the administrative/political decision-maker and to the judge is quite severe, as we have suggested. Although the former is able to seek information across a wide spectrum of sources and can make use of any form of information that might be of benefit, the judicial policy-maker is more restricted in the means by which to gather and introduce various forms of information into legal proceedings. And although the former is allowed to consider as many associated questions as believed necessary, the judicial machinery is basically a legal forum where regulations all force a convergence of attention toward the specific act or acts basic to the litigation. And finally, although the former can take into account a variety of political and/or social consequences of the decision to be made, the court is restricted to certain prescribed norms of remedy that may generate a variety of unpopular or unanticipated consequences, but that cannot be avoided. Although administrative/political decision-makers have available to them an approach emphasizing flexibility and the necessity of taking into account a variety of information sources, the courts must adhere to established channels of fact finding and must guide their own decisions on the countless previous cases that have relevant precedent.

Now that we have presented what may be termed the more "traditional" understanding of the latitude of the courts in fact finding, we must note immediately that the content, form, and breadth of information coming into legal proceedings are changing rapidly. The two areas where change is most evident (and would be most expected) are those of describing the extent of injury and fashioning an appropriate remedy. Although even traditional litigation models have recognized the somewhat broader latitude necessary in these areas, the current changes are moving considerably beyond former boundaries.

The delineation of a legally recognizable injury is more closely tied to the legal elements of litigation than is remedy formulation. This is because the injury in question must relate to the original cause of action. That is, the causal relation between the wrong complained of and the present injury to the complaining party must be made explicit. Furthermore, since the injury must violate one or more legal rights of a person, there is the further need to show a causal connection between rights and injury. What is emerging is the development of analyses within courtrooms that seek to combine scientifically valid testimony on the causality of act and injury with the legal analysis of public rights and personal injury. The combination of social science data and legal interpretations of the Fourteenth Amendment with respect to school segregation is but one relevant example. Here what has been necessary is not only to establish the nature of the injuries suffered as a result of *de jure* segregation by the children involved, but also to show that such injuries result as the deliberate and willful acts of public officials.

School desegregation may be a bit too stark as an example. The complexities of other educational ligitation have seldom had such visible manifestations of the outcomes of official decision-making as we find with the blatant efforts to maintain dual schools. In many other cases, it is often necessary to make assumptions about the nature of education and its intended outcomes. If such questions are seldom clear in pedagogical circles, imagine attempting to sustain a particular view in the structured setting of the courtroom. For example, in attempting to demonstrate that missing a certain number of days of school, or being taught in one manner as opposed to another, or being placed in one classroom as opposed to another results in an injury to one's rights to particular educational benefits, it becomes necessary first to define clearly the intended benefit and, second, to show that the student was substantially denied such a benefit.

It should be apparent that answers to questions such as these are essentially answers to fundamental issues of education. What are appropriate educational benefits? How are such benefits measured? When do we know a student has been denied such benefits? Much social science data have been introduced in an effort to answer such questions, but they have yet to be resolved with any consistency or certainty. In this instance, the tenuous use of social science data becomes apparent—as does the very basis of relying on the courts to provide educational policy guidance. But as we also noted earlier, where else might we turn? We can offer no legitimate substitute.

It is when the courts turn to the fashioning of a remedy that they are most able to make use of a wide range of information forms. In the effort to devise an equitable solution to the wrong committed, the courts can seek expert guidance, consultants, findings from commissions, reports, and other such resources. When the end goal is a response to the litigation at hand, the means at the disposal of the courts are broader than at any other time during the proceedings. Among all the reasons for seeking an effective remedy, one that always has high saliency is that only cursory attention to a remedy and its resultant failure may well result in the case's reappearing in the courts for another round of adjudication. By seeking to devise a remedy that solves the problem to the satisfaction of the parties and that goes beyond standard law-based remedies, the courts are, in this sense, more activist than they were only a short time ago.

The information needs of the court during the remedy stage are specific to the issue at hand. The remedy stage is not one where grand theories or philosophic notions of distributive justice can be applied without the transformation into concrete actions available to the courts. And although the social sciences are frequently accused of being too theoretical for the practical aspects of social life, it is in the remedy stage that research efforts can be brought to bear.[2] Even if data on what does work for a particular set of circumstances are relatively scarce, the social sciences should be able to provide an assessment of what would most likely not work as an effective remedy. At the stage of fashioning a remedy, the courts are in need of the best information they can secure. Without such inputs, the judge is left with less powerful and effective interventions—and an ongoing series of litigations to ensure compliance with the legal principles involved.

The needs of the courts suggest that it is worthy of social scientists' consideration to link basic to applied research efforts more closely. Although social scientists may be little concerned with the legal precedents or issues involved, they should recognize that the courts are now directing the educational systems of this country in a way that research results of themselves seldom, if ever, could. Thus the courts are providing a vehicle by which to transform an integral aspect of American society. For those who wish not only to understand society, but to better it, directing their efforts toward the generation of knowledge that will benefit to the courts would be no small contribution.

On The Present Volume

A central theme of all the papers presented here is that the courts are playing an increasing role in the formulation of educational policy at the local, state, and federal levels. With this shift, significant aspects of policy-making for American education are now derived from the courtrooms rather than from boardrooms or even classrooms. There is also entailed in this transition a re-interpretation of the critical issues from a pedagogical framework to a legal one. As will be suggested more than once in the pages to follow, it is yet an open question as to the long-term costs and benefits not only of changing substantive interpretations of pressing issues in education, but of changing the very means by which they are resolved.

Recognizing the dimensions and implications of this emerging situation in American education, the National Institute of Education, Department of Health, Education, and Welfare, convened an international symposium, "Education, Social Science, and the Judicial Process," in February 1976. The focus of the symposium was an exploration of the manner in which the definitions of educational problems, the form and content of social science data brought to bear upon an understanding of these problems, and the resultant policy decisions have been influenced by the new role of the courts.

The seven papers that follow were presented at that symposium. The co-editors of this volume also served as the conference co-convenors. More than 700 social scientists, lawyers, judges, educators, school administrators, governmental officials, and others concerned with educational matters were in attendance. The international dimension of the symposium was reflected in the six countries that were represented: Australia, Canada, Federal Republic of Germany, Mexico, the United Kingdom, and the United States. As was made evident in countless conversations, the transition of educational decision-making into the legal arena is not a phenomenon restricted to the United States, but one present in varying degrees in other countries as well.

Notes

[1]Herbert L. Costner, De Tocqueville on equality, 19 *Pacific Sociological Review* 425-426 (1976).

[2]The paper by Federal District Court Judge William Doyle in the present volume expands greatly upon this role for the social sciences as an aid to the courts at the remedy stage.

Contributors

Ronald J. Anson studied at Columbia University and the University of Colorado, where he received his J.D. degree. He has been a research analyst at the National Institute of Education since its creation in 1972, researching legal and policy questions in the area of law and education and initiating a broad range of sociolegal research at the Institute. He is co-editor of *Students' Right to Due Process: Professional Discretion and Liability Under Goss and Wood*, and has written various articles on law and education.

Julius L. Chambers received his undergraduate training in history at North Carolina Central University, and began his study of law at the University of North Carolina in 1959. He graduated Juris Doctor with High Honors in 1962. The following year, he received the LL.M. degree from the Columbia University School of Law. Since he entered law practice in Charlotte, North Carolina, in 1964, he has been involved in numerous civil rights cases. He is presently a Lecturer at the University of Pennsylvania Law School, and is also President of the NAACP Legal Defense and Educational Fund, Inc.

Kenneth B. Clark received his Ph.D. in social psychology from Columbia University. He is a Distinguished Professor of Psychology Emeritus of the City College of the City University of New York and recently retired as President of the Metropolitan Applied Research Center, Inc. He has served as a consultant to numerous foundations, universities, and private corporations and to the U.S. government. He is the author of many books and articles, including the prize-winning volume *Dark Ghetto* (1965), *A Relevant War Against Poverty* (1968), and *Pathos of Power* (1974). His early work received national prominence with its citation by the United States Supreme Court in its 1954 *Brown v. Board of Education* decision.

David K. Cohen is presently Professor of Education and Social Policy in the Harvard Graduate School of Education, and was previously a Visiting Fellow at the Joint Center for Urban Studies of Harvard and M.I.T. He was also on the staff of the U.S. Commission on Civil Rights, where he was director of research for the report, *Racial Isolation in the Public Schools* (1967). He has published widely in a variety of journals, including *U.C.L.A. Law Review, Saturday Review, Commentary, American Journal of Sociology*, and the *Harvard Educational Review*. He is also a coauthor with Christopher Jencks and others of the widely discussed book *Inequality: A Reassessment of the Effects of Family and Schooling in America* (1973).

John L. Coons received his law degree from Northwestern University and is currently Professor of Law at the University of California, Berkeley, and co-principal investigator of the Childhood and Government Project at Berkeley. He has been actively involved in the California school finance case, *Serrano v. Priest*, helping to formulate the constitutional norms and practical remedies needed in the case. In his association with the Childhood and Government Project, Professor Coons has been involved in a wide variety of socio-legal research centering on the rights and status of children in society. This concern is paralleled by his teaching of social sciences and the law. He has written a number of articles and books, including *Private Wealth and Public Education* (1970), which is used as a conceptual framework for school finance reform litigation cases throughout the country.

William E. Doyle, United States Circuit Judge for the Tenth Circuit, received his law degree with honors from George Washington University, then returned to Colorado to practice law. He has served on the Supreme Court of Colorado, the United States District Court, and the United States Court of Appeals for the Tenth District. He has also been a professor of law and written articles for a number of legal journals. His duties on the Tenth Circuit bench have included one of the first major northern desegregation cases, *Keyes v. School District No. 1, Denver, Colorado*.

Ronald M. Dworkin currently occupies the Chair of Jurisprudence at Oxford University, previously occupied by H. L. A. Hart. Professor Dworkin graduated from Harvard College and Harvard Law School, was a Rhodes Scholar at Oxford, and worked as a practicing attorney before beginning his teaching career. He was Hohfeld Professor of Jurisprudence at Yale Law School and remains on the faculties of New York University Law School and Cornell University. His writing appears in a wide variety of legal and philosophical journals and covers questions of legal, political, and moral philosophy.

Ray C. Rist is a Senior Fulbright Fellow at the Max Planck Institut in Berlin and at the University of Bonn during the 1976-1977 academic year. He previously served as Senior Policy Analyst, as Head of the Desegregation Studies Division, and as Acting Associate Director of the National Institute of Education, U.S. Department of Health, Education, and Welfare. Rist is the author of *The Urban School: A*

Factory for Failure (1973) and *The Invisible Children: A Study of School Integration* (1977); he has also published numerous articles and contributed to several books. He was educated at Valparaiso University and Washington University, from which he received his Ph.D. in 1970.

Janet A. Weiss is a graduate student in the Department of Psychology and Social Relations, Harvard University, and expects to receive a Ph.D. in social psychology in 1977. Her current research is focused on the use of information in judgment and decision-making. She is particularly interested in the use of social science information in decisions made by public policy-makers. Her publications include "Using Social Science for Social Policy," which appeared in the Spring 1976 issue of *Policy Studies Journal.*

Eleanor P. Wolf received her Ph.D. in sociology from Wayne State University in 1959. Prior to that time, she was Director of the Michigan Labor Committee for Human Rights and a Visiting Professor at the Merrill-Palmer Institute. She serves as a consultant to numerous organizations in the areas of race, education, and labor, and has written widely in such journals as *Phylon, Journal of Social Issues, The Public Interest,* and *Race.* She has also completed a large-scale study of racial transition in urban neighborhoods, which culminated in the book *Change and Renewal in an Urban Community* (1969) with Charles Lebeaux. Her recent research on the utilization of social science materials in school desegregation proceedings has been supported by the Ford Foundation.

Contents

Social Science, Constitutional Rights, and The Courts

Kenneth B. Clark

In a recently published book, *Affirmative Discrimination,* Nathan Glazer concluded his discussion of the issue of busing with the Olympian decision:

> . . . the judges have gone far beyond what the Constitution can reasonably be thought to allow or require in the operation of this complex process. The judges should now stand back and allow the forces of political democracy in a pluralist society to do their proper work.[1]

This statement is startling. When analyzed, it becomes clear that, in the calm and balanced tone acceptable to academia, Glazer is proposing a radical repudiation of a major contribution of the American Constitutional system. For two hundred years, a system of checks and balances has protected America from the more flagrant abuses of power concentrations—and has protected the minorities from the tyranny of the majority.

One can only conclude that the shocking implications of Glazer's proposal are obscured by the fact that it is compatible with the current fashionable "neoliberal revisionism" that dominates the thoughts and utterances of a well-publicized group of social scientists. In trying to understand the argument presented by Professor Glazer's provocatively entitled book, one initially associates it with the controversial "benign neglect" memorandum of Daniel P. Moynihan. This is not surprising, in view of the fact that Moynihan and Glazer collaborated on *Beyond the Melting Pot* and subsequent articles, wherein the concept of the validity and the virtue of ethnic pluralism was elaborated. The thesis that American democracy requires various ethnic groups to wait their turn in the process of eventually enjoying the benefits and protection of our system was presented as a matter of historical practicality if not of morality and justice.

1

As one speculates about the meaning of Glazer's proposal—that the rights of minorities should be determined by the will of the majority, which historically has restricted these rights—one is tempted to become fascinated with such abstract academic seminar questions as the relationship between the Glazer-Moynihan pragmatic concept of constitutional rights—the complex problem of remedying long-standing racial injustices—and the fashionable notion of moral relativism that was so dominant in social science thinking in the 1930's and 1940's. Indeed, if one succumbed to this temptation to deal with this problem within the framework of academic abstractions, one would be reminded that Ernest van den Haag was the first social scientist to criticize publicly the role and findings of those social scientists who were involved as expert witnesses in the public school desegregation cases that led to the *Brown* decision of 1954. Without waiting for it to become fashionable among his social science colleagues, van den Haag insisted that the social science evidence collected and analyzed for these cases was weak and flimsy, and certainly did not support the contention that racial segregation in the society and racially segregated schools damaged the personalities of American children. He stated:

> Whether humiliation leaves deep and lasting traces and whether it increases the incidence of personality disorders among Negroes, we do not know (nor do we know whether congregation would obviate them).
> The "scientific" evidence for the injury is no more "scientific" than the evidence presented in favor of racial prejudice . . . .[2]

Looking back upon my own debates with van den Haag twenty years ago, and comparing my attitudes and impressions at that time with my feelings and reactions to the current group of social science racial and ethnic revisionists, I must confess that I had a more positive professional reaction to the direct, candid, forthright, negative reaction to the *Brown* decision as expressed by Professor van den Haag than I now have to the rather circuitous and seemingly more sophisticated position of contemporary social scientists. Today those social scientists who are opposed to the spirit and the implementation of the *Brown* decision tend to deny that they are opposed to racial discrimination and segregation but, at the same time, they insist that attempts to remedy these inequities are undemocratic or will make matters worse. They assert that attempts to remedy racial segregation in housing will encourage white flight and thereby increase segregation. They argue that attempts to enforce the *Brown* decision and to protect the constitutional rights of minority children against being damaged in racially segregated schools in northern urban centers are unrealistic, will increase racial polarization, will encourage white flight, and will eventually result in the abandonment of America's major cities to poor, unstable, and crime-prone minorities. Their arguments have been widely publicized. In fact it appears as if a large percentage, if not the majority, of the American press and media have accepted these arguments as realistic and practical. Probably a majority of the well-informed American public has been made to believe that these opinions are given validity by systematic social science findings.

The most widely publicized recent example of social science revisionism and neoliberalism is in the statements and discussions of Coleman's alleged change in his opinions, attitudes, and conclusions about the advisability of desegregating American public schools through the reassignment of pupils and, if necessary, providing transportation for the reassigned pupils. It is generally believed that in his original report, *Equality of Educational Opportunity,* published in 1966, Coleman advocated desegregation of the schools and favored busing.[3] In a series of public interviews concerning the findings and implications of his most recent study, Coleman is presented as having changed his position on this issue. He has stated, among other things, the following:

1. That he has conducted research and obtained data that show that court-ordered busing for the purpose of public school desegregation resulted in the flight of the white middle class from American cities.[4]
2. That federal courts, by ordering desegregation of public schools in opposition to the will of the majority of whites, are contributing to racial tensions.[5]
3. More specifically, that the federal courts are "the worst of all possible instruments for carrying out a very sensitive activity like integration of the schools."[6]

In one of the most important of these interviews, Professor Coleman admitted to a reporter of *The New York Times* "that his public comments went beyond the scientific data he had gathered . . . he said that his study did not deal with housing, and that his arguments applied to trends in only two or three southern cities."[7]

What Coleman did not state in this partial concession of scientific default was the equally important fact that his recent research provided him with absolutely no data to support his contention that the federal courts and judges are "the worst of all possible instruments for carrying out a very sensitive activity like integration of the schools."

There are many similarities between the present positions of Coleman and Glazer. There are also some important differences. Probably the most significant difference is that, for the most part, Glazer, Moynihan, Daniel Bell, and other social scientists who have been published in such magazines as *The Public Interest* and *Commentary* and who have written books on racial and social policy issues, have written what are essentially essays. They have exercised their constitutional right of freedom to express their personal opinions, biases, theories, and analyses, but generally have not deliberately sought to tie their personal opinions and impressions to objective research and systematic empirical findings. For example, Glazer's latest book, *Affirmative Discrimination,* is essentially a collection of essays consistent with the articles he has published in *Commentary.* His allies and his critics are free to agree or disagree with his opinions and conclusions. Coleman, on the other hand, clearly asserted initially that his conclusions concerning the detrimental consequences of busing came directly from his empirical research. This, without question, is misleading to the general public and to his professional colleagues.

One could argue that, in his eventual admission that he had gone beyond his findings in his anti-busing statements, Coleman had erased any reasonable basis by which his critics could charge him with a willful violation of a fundamental principle of scientific integrity. Personally, I do not accept this. My criticism of Coleman may seem to some reasonable observers as unnecessarily harsh. It is possible that the severity of my judgment of Coleman on this critical issue of racial justice and social policy may be attributed to the fact that I, as a social scientist, have been aligned with those social scientists and American citizens who have insisted that racial justice in America is irrevocably tied to the desegregation of our schools and that racial integration in all aspects of American society must be an unqualified goal if American democracy is to be worthy of respect rather than of mere rhetoric. It is also a fact that I am a social psychologist who happens to be black. I nonetheless contend, without apology, that James Coleman, in his recent public utterances, has deliberately misled the American public and has used his status and his prestige as a publicized social scientist as a forum from which he now projects his personal biases. This violates the most fundamental principle governing that unquestioned sense of trust essential in the ongoing and challenging struggle for scientific truth. Certainly any physical scientist in his biochemical research who made public statements that transcended reasonable interpretation of his findings would be censured by his colleagues and professional associations.

If this opinion is correct, then an equally serious problem is posed by the fact that Coleman's colleagues in the social sciences have not publicly raised questions about the propriety of his recent public utterances and, as far as I know, have not yet called Coleman to account for or to explain his position on this matter. Of course, this issue must be explored responsibly with all the necessary safeguards essential for academic and scientific freedom of inquiry and the rights of American citizens to think and speak freely. Until Coleman's colleagues decide to explore this matter with the seriousness and objectivity it deserves, one is forced to speculate on the possibility that the extensive publicizing of a social scientist—the granting of interviews to newspapers, magazines, and radio and television talk shows—will automatically give immunity from questioning the scientific propriety and integrity of any social scientist who has achieved such celebrity status. Given the realities of social and political power as it operates in a dynamic social system, one could state the related hypothesis that such unquestioned immunity is more likely to be granted to those social science celebrities who expound a point of view that supports the status quo and who are not clearly aligned with those citizens and government officials who are seeking racial and social justice.

On the other hand, those social scientists whose values require them to be openly aligned with those who are part of the ongoing struggle for racial and social justice are more likely to be required to meet the most severe tests of scientific integrity and personal probity.

Aside from these important specific problems raised by the recent activities and utterances of the neoliberal social science revisionists, a most important question emerges with complex starkness: What is the present role of social scientists in the general area of social policy and, more specifically, in the immediate social policy problem of seeking to implement the adjudicated constitutional rights of minorities in the United States?

In the optimism of the early 1950's—an optimism I not only shared but participated in with enthusiasm—social scientists, with a few exceptions, tended to accept uncritically the belief that they not only had a role but the obligation to organize, interpret, and make available to policy-makers—the legislative, executive, and judicial branches of state and federal governments—social science data that bore directly or indirectly on social issues. In the area of race relations in America, the optimism of the late 1940's and 1950's seemed based on the fact that social scientists were generally developing methods and perspectives that were making important research-based contributions to the understanding of American race relations. The contributions of such distinguished social scientists as Louis Worth, Howard Odum, Franz Boaz, E. Franklin Frazier, Charles Johnson, Otto Klineberg, Gordon Allport, and many others marked the high point of a positive collaboration of social science and social policy toward the goals of racial justice. Gunnar Myrdal's and his associates' classic study of the American race problem, published in the early 1940's under the title *An American Dilemma,* can be viewed as the inevitable culmination of this positive ferment and natural collaboration of social science with the forces of social justice in America.[8] Footnote 11 in the *Brown* decision of 1954 could then be viewed as the ultimate demonstration of this joint enterprise. Upon the basis of these indications, one could argue that social science was as necessary for the development of stable and rational social policy and racial justice as the biological sciences were essential for the development of an effective medical technology.

I made this argument twenty years ago in my response to the criticism of the late Edmond Cahn, Distinguished Professor of Jurisprudence at the New York University Law School. Cahn was highly critical of the role of social scientists in public school desegregation cases. The most important critical point he made in his discussion of the role of social scientists in the *Brown* decision was his contention that the United States Supreme Court should not base the protection of the constitutional rights of American citizens on what he considered the flimsy evidence of social scientists. At that time I stated "one must take seriously his [Professor Cahn's] argument that the constitutional rights of Negroes or other Americans should not rest on social scientists' testimony alone. If he had concentrated and elaborated on this issue on a high level of academic discourse, he might have made an important contribution to thought in a field in which he is competent." This prophetic statement was followed by my recognition of the fact, even in the period of optimism twenty years ago, that:

> Social scientists, like other knowledgeable individuals in our society, must be sensitive to the problems of power and the techniques of social control which are operative in the society in which they work. In spite of the demand for objectivity and integrity in the search for truth, the important determinant of serious scientific work, social scientists are influenced indirectly and sometimes directly, subtly and sometimes crudely, by the prevailing social biases and uncritically accepted frames of reference of their society.[9]

I concluded that essay as follows:

> Those who attempt to use the methods of social science in dealing with problems which threaten the status quo must realistically expect retaliatory attacks, direct or oblique, and must be prepared to accept the risks which this role inevitably involves. Attacks motivated by understandable political opposition or the criticisms which reflect the vested interest or limitations of other disciplines must be expected. Differences of opinion and interpretation concerning the relative weight to be given to the available evidence must, of course, be expected among conscientious social scientists. In this latter instance, however, certain fundamental rules of social scholarship, consistency and logic must prevail if the controversy is to be intellectually constructive and socially beneficial.
>
> It is a fact that the collaboration between psychologists and other social scientists which culminated in the *Brown* decision will continue in spite of criticisms. Those who question the propriety of this collaboration will

probably increase the intensity of their criticism—particularly as social controversy and conflict increase. Nevertheless, some social scientists will continue to play a role in this aspect of the legal and judicial process because as scientists they cannot do otherwise. They are obligated by temperament, moral commitment and their concept of the role and demands of science. They will do so because they see the valid goals of the law, government, social institutions, religion and science as identical; namely to secure for man personal fulfillment in a just, stable and viable society.[10]

Recent facts have put my earlier debate with Professor Cahn in a different context. Today we are confronted with the anomaly that a Distinguished Professor at Harvard Law School, Derrick Bell, who happens to be black, has gone beyond the serious questions raised by Professor Cahn twenty years ago and is now publicly insisting that attempts to desegregate public schools in American cities are wrong and that in fact the repeal of *Plessy v. Ferguson* by *Brown* is a serious practical, if not judicial, mistake. My analysis of Professor Bell's position is that it is the legal form of what I call the social science revisionism personified by Glazer, Coleman, and those who share their point of view.

The climate within which the school desegregation controversy now exists is without question observably different from the 1950's and the ten-year period immediately following the *Brown* decision. The center of gravity of the civil rights movement and the public school desegregation tensions have moved from the southern states to northern urban communities. With this movement, northern whites have developed more sophisticated forms of evasion of the *Brown* decision. Among their most powerful allies are social scientists and some formerly liberal lawyers. In the North, realistic politicians are not required to make the flamboyant statements of resistance that characterized the political postures of white southern officials fifteen or twenty years ago. Educators who had always played a minor, if not negative, role in the struggle for school desegregation in the South are at best silent, if not equivocating or negative, when confronted with the problem in northern cities. Nor are the churches and religious leaders particularly inclined to assume public and assertive leadership in seeking to help American education move from the anachronism and human damage associated with racially segregated schools. "Realistic" elected political officials, school boards, city councils, state legislators, and congressmen understandably became responsive to the major white opposition to any serious attempt to implement the *Brown* decision in northern cities. Sophisticated, semantic forms of evasion and inaction supplanted the southern forms of histrionic defiance. The northern approach to a functional repeal of *Brown* relied on such semantic strategies as the claim for being in favor of the desegregation of schools provided one did not make any serious attempt to desegregate the schools. Those who insisted that the *Brown* decision applied as much to New York, Chicago, Boston, and Los Angeles as it did to Little Rock, Birmingham, and Charleston were dismissed as unrealistic if not racial agitators.

The spurious anti-busing issue became and remains a major and, so far, successful political device for blocking effective desegregation. Recently, a Congressman from New York State visited my office and sought to enlist my support as a Member of the New York Board of Regents in getting the Commissioner of Education in the State of New York to rescind a high school desegregation order in New York City. It was clear, even to this Congressman, that there was absolutely no busing issue involved here. Instead he raised the argument that attempts to desegregate the high schools in New York City would precipitate white flight. He prefaced his attempt to persuade me to join him in rejecting the orders of the Commissioner by stating with intensity that he was a liberal and that he was in favor of integration. What he did not state, but what was implied in his presentation, was that he was in favor of integration of the public schools as long as it did not irritate and inconvenience middle-class whites.

Within this present context, therefore, it is clear that only the federal courts *can* be charged with the responsibility of protecting the constitutional rights of minorities and enforcing the clear and explicit mandate of the *Brown* decision. Present realities have made it clear to even the most optimistic social scientists that the roots of American racism go deep and involve all areas—North, South, East, and West—of this nation. The majority of American whites, particularly northerners, now oppose all attempts to comply with the letter and the spirit of the *Brown* decision. If the issue of the desegregation of the public schools were put to a referendum now, twenty years after that historic decision, the chances are that it would be defeated. But this should not be surprising. If this were not so, there would have been no need to take these cases before the federal courts. The present controversies centering around the implementation of the *Brown* decision in northern cities make even more clear the keystone fact of the American democratic system: that a critical function of the federal courts is to protect the constitutional rights of American minorities, particularly when those rights are being opposed or in any way qualified or threatened by the majority. The key message, the innovating rationale of the American Constitution, is that a stable democracy cannot permit tyranny of the majority. If there were no need for effective checks and balances on the power of the majority, there would be no need for a federal judicial system.

It is difficult to believe that the present group of social scientists, the neoliberal revisionists, are not aware of the fact that, in counseling that the constitutional rights of Negro children be determined by the attitudes of the white majority rather than by the courts, they are in fact arguing that these constitutional rights be denied. They know and they assert that these rights are opposed by the majority. Theirs is the realism of anarchy, which is indistinguishable from racial immorality.

In the earlier struggles for social and racial justice, when social scientists joined with concerned citizens in the attempt to strengthen American democracy, there was hope and identification with the eventual fulfillment of American ideals for all. In the partnership with lawyers and policy-makers toward these goals, social scientists were proud of their role. Their values and compatible roles gave substance to their belief that, in seeking justice for minorities, they were strengthening American democracy for the benefit of all human beings.

The perspective of the neoliberal revisionist social scientists has made it clear that now in matters of social equity and in the ongoing struggle for racial justice, concerned citizens must put their faith and trust in our federal courts. Professor Edmond Cahn's critical prophecy twenty years ago now seems confirmed. The business of social justice is too important to be left in the hands of those "social scientists" who are primarily responsive to majority fashion, prejudices, and power.

Notes

[1]Nathan Glazer, *Affirmative Discrimination: Ethnic Inequality and Public Policy* (New York: Basic Books, 1975), p. 129.

[2]Ralph Ross and Ernest van den Haag, *Fabric of Society* (New York: Harcourt Brace, 1957), Appendix: Prejudice about prejudice, pp. 165-166.

[3]James S. Coleman, *et al.*, *Equality of Educational Opportunity* (Washington, D.C.: U.S. Department of Health, Education, and Welfare, Office of Education, 1966).

[4]James S. Coleman, Racial segregation in the schools: new research with new policy implications, 57 *Phi Delta Kappan* 75-78 (1975).

[5]William Grant, Sociologist's busing switch based on questionable data, *Detroit Free Press*, August 19, 1975, p. 3.

[6]*National Observer*, June 7, 1975, p. 18.

[7]Robert Reinhold, Coleman concedes views exceeded his race data, *The New York Times*, July 11, 1975, p. 1.

[8]Gunnar Myrdal, *et al.*, *An American Dilemma* (New York: Harper, 1944).

[9]Kenneth B. Clark, The desegregation case: criticism of the social scientists' role, 5 *Villanova Law Review* 224-240 (1959).

[10]*Ibid.*

Social Science Evidence in Court Cases

William E. Doyle*

Comments on Perspective and Context

My exact topic is, "Can social science data be used in judicial decision-making?"

The answer to that question is that social science data or other evidence are less important in judicial decision-making in the field of constitutional law than most people think. Such data are also even less controversial than people might think. The more controversial issue is whether courts should even be considering cases that might require or produce social science evidence. The foes of so-called judicial activism would say the courts ought to get out, but even where the decision is against this participation it is a social science decision. Courts do not, of course, have a roving commission to hear and decide controverted issues of social policy, nor do they relish such efforts. Most judges would prefer more traditional cases, which call on their legal skills. But just as the judge is unable to select the cases he prefers, neither can he eschew the cases he does not prefer.

Congress is the main culprit. It has required the federal courts to hear policy cases having social science aspects in numerous instances. Claims of citizens raising what might be called social policy disputes have been delegated to the courts for at least a century. The Civil Rights Act of 1871,[1] for example, gave access to the federal courts for citizens seeking "to redress the deprivation, under color of any state law . . . of any right, privilege, or immunity secured by the Constitution . . . or any Act of Congress providing for equal rights. . . ." In the 1960's, in the form of Title VII of the Civil Rights Act of 1964,[2] Congress required the courts to shoulder part of the burden of

*I have had law clerk assistance from Jeffrey N. Gordon.

policing private employment practices against racial discrimination. The problem of judicial involvement in social policy is thus a matter of long standing.

Given that federal courts must hear disputes involving issues of social policy, it is not surprising that the parties trying the cases offer so-called "social science" evidence. Judges must receive and hear all relevant and competent evidence presented by the parties to a lawsuit. As Justice Brandeis once wrote, judicial decision "should be based upon a consideration of relevant facts, actual or possible—*Ex facto jus oritur.** That ancient rule must prevail in order that we may have a system of living law."[3]

The weighing and sifting of social science data is not then a new task that judges of this generation have taken upon themselves. The tasks have resulted from Congressional authorization. Further, the cases in the first third of this century considering the power of the states to pass economic and social welfare legislation commonly involved social science data.[4] In fact, it was only after courts began taking such data seriously that the kind of socially protective legislation that we today take for granted was able to withstand judicial scrutiny.[5] A brief in a 1908 case, one of the first instances in which the Supreme Court upheld laws prescribing maximum working hours, consisted of two pages of legal argument and 111 pages of surveys, government statistics, factory reports, medical discussion, and employer/employee opinion samples.[6] From this a whole jurisprudential school has taken form, as a result of which there has developed judicial recognition of social science factors. This school was dubbed "Sociological Jurisprudence" in a 1911 article by Roscoe Pound.[7]

Let us consider another example. The Sherman Act, a major piece of antitrust legislation passed in 1890,[8] made unlawful all "unreasonable" restraints of trade. It has fallen to the courts ever since to try to fashion a workable definition of "reasonableness" in various business settings.[9] The courts have quite freely employed economic and other social science data and analysis in deciding such cases.[10] In more recent times, the Supreme Court has expressly considered social science data in cases considering the choice between six person and twelve person juries,[11] the deterrent effectiveness and popular acceptance of the death penalty,[12] whether alcoholism[13] or narcotics addiction[14] should be regarded as diseases, whether financing schools through property taxes necessarily leads to disparity in education resources,[15] and what, under contemporary standards, counts as obscenity.[16] And, as noted above, Congress put the courts directly in a social science area, that of considering various kinds of social data—the utility of certain employment tests, statistical inferences of discrimination in employment—when it passed Title VII.[17]

*"The law arises out of the fact."

So, when people raise a hue and cry in emotional cases such as school desegregation litigation against courts' considering social science data, they commonly have in mind an objection to courts' using social science data in the context of particular cases, and this is especially so if the decisions are contrary to their personal view. A popular view is that the studies of a few psychologists and sociologists are the source of all social woes, and worse, other sociologists and psychologists say those studies are misleading and inaccurate. Of course, this group is not necessarily consistent in its criticism: having complained about the courts' use of social science as a basis for unpopular decisions, some urge on the court other, allegedly contrary, social science data, so as to persuade a retreat.

These objections, I think, are based on a misunderstanding of the very limited consideration given to social science evidence in court deliberation and the limited role such evidence plays in the outcome.

Far more important than social science evidence in policy cases, e.g., a school desegregation case, is the basic law that has been referred to. The decisive factor is the Constitution of the United States, which protects *all* citizens from violation of their rights by state legislatures or other policy-making agencies of the state. The elements considered in making this decision are the wording of the Constitution, sometimes history, precedent in the form of court decisions, reason, and moral law or natural law. But contrary to popular thinking, the desire of the court to engage in social engineering is not a factor.

Social Science Evidence in Determining Liability in a Constitutional Law Case

A good illustration of the workings of the judicial process in the public *policy* type of case is found in the Supreme Court's decision in *Brown v. Board of Education*,[18] which is a fundamental authority, because this case, among other things, changed the doctrine that had prevailed for almost 60 years: schools that were separate but equal satisfied the Constitution. This rule, first expounded in *Plessy v. Ferguson*,[19] was repudiated in *Brown v. Board of Education*. The *Brown* case condemned as unconstitutional the segregation of races as a result of state action. This basic legal principle was not founded on social science data, nor is it open to being refuted by social science evidence, and therefore this kind of evidence has little value in determining whether the segregation is actionable.[20]

Conceivably, social science data could come into play in connection with the intent with which a school board acted. Thus, the official actions of the school board can be and frequently are scrutinized carefully to determine whether it acted with an intent to isolate minority students from

Anglo students. If the school board has jockeyed boundaries with the apparent aim of concentrating minorities within a school attendance area, it would follow that such gerrymandering is *de jure*.[21] This kind of data is entirely unrelated to social science theory or social science opinion (such as the notion that school desegregation improves achievement scores). But the lesson of *Brown* has little to do with achievement scores. Rather, the key is that the isolation of an entire people is constitutionally wrong—is repugnant also to our most fundamental belief, to our fundamental notion of democracy. No person would argue that any race or group is inferior to another, that it is to be considered unworthy to associate with the excluding group. I submit then that this is the actual key to the *Brown* decision. This viewpoint no doubt evolved and finally emerged long after the date of the adoption of the Fourteenth Amendment, which contains the guarantee of equality under the laws.

The reader is apt to object to the foregoing analysis by saying, "Didn't the Supreme Court base its holding in *Brown* that 'separate educational facilities are inherently unequal' *on social science* studies that black children were in fact harmed by segregation? Isn't *Brown* based on findings of the power of segregation to create negative self-image among minority children?"[22] The answer to both questions is "no." *Brown* and the cases that follow—*Green County, Swann,* and *Keyes*—were not predicated on the studies of sociologists and psychologists. They are all based on the fundamental invalidity of isolating a people from other people; that the ideal of *Plessy*—separate but equal—had not been attainable and never would be. Although then there remains a temptation to see *Brown* and the school cases that follow as being based on social science data, it is clear that it and its progeny are founded on much more fundamental precepts—organic, moral, positive law, and reason.[23]

Those who claim that social science is a decisive factor overlook the fact that the United States is held together and governed by a Constitution, which comprises organic and fundamental law embodied in a written document that places limits on state power and guarantees individual liberty. Included are broad phrases—"equal protection," "due process," "freedom of speech," "cruel and unusual punishment"—that, if they are to have the power to "secure the Blessings of Liberty to ourselves and our Posterity," must be interpreted and applied to concrete situations. Throughout most of the two centuries of our national existence, the courts have been recognized as the authoritative expositors of what the Constitution requires. The recognition of the courts' role is founded on the fact that, of the three departments of government, the Judicial branch is the only one that can take a detached view in construing the Constitution, and also because institutions of majority-rule government cannot always be relied on to protect minority rights. If the Constitution is to afford protection to all—for we are all the minority sometimes—its interpretation must be free of popular pressures. Decision-making in this area has a social science quality, but it is not the same subject we are presently discussing.

Yet it is generally recognized that decision-making in this area is often controversial. This is because there are at least two schools of thought—one that favors giving effect to the constitutional principle and one that disfavors its recognition. On occasion, the courts may harken back to the clearly-expressed intentions of the Framers, and we can acknowledge with confidence that the courts are only referring to choices that undeniably are embedded in the Constitution. Yet in most cases that interpret the broad phrases of the Constitution, such as equal protection, the value choice the courts must make will not find universal or even majority acceptance. The lingering suspicion—created by the act of constitutional interpretation—is that constitutional adjudication is only the imposition of the judge's decision over the will of at least some of the people.

The fact that concepts evolve and changes occur does not mean that the changes are based on the view of any particular sociology. It more likely means that the particular controversy has brought the constitutional provision into sharper and clearer focus. It possibly means also that the rule or principle has evolved through the customs and mores stages and has achieved the general recognition that results in its adoption. Constitutional decisions are also, it is true, the product of particular facts. Consider, for example, the individual facts of the individual cases that were consolidated in *Brown v. Board*. All this, however, is different from saying that rulings stand or fall on the continued viability of some sociological opinion. This brings to mind the very recent expressions by James Coleman, which statements differed from his prior extensive research. We will not go into the much debated merits of Coleman's recent study. We merely cite this to illustrate the hazard that would exist in changing the ruling on the basis of current changes of viewpoint, however authoritative such opinions might be.[24]

In sum, then, courts do not take social science facts as the touchstone of constitutional interpretation because such data are adjective rather than substantive in nature. Such material is alien to the constitutional law decision. Research assumptions and methodologies are apt to be held defective and social attitudes and reactions—the very data that social science research purports to collect and analyze—may also change. The courts' constitutional adjudications are based on positive law that is embodied in the Constitution and prior decisions rather than on the most recent published social science study. Reliance on the constitutional interpretation that isolation of minorities is inherently unequal and discriminatory has more quality if backed by reason, history, and experience as gleaned from prior decisions.

The Supreme Court's statement that "separate is inherently unequal" is an act of constitutional interpretation giving life to the concept of the equal protection clause; it is an attempt to infuse meaning into a "Constitution intended to endure for ages to come." We would pose a greater danger to our 200-year experience in constitutional democracy if we were to rest constitutional interpretation on social science data rather than on the bedrock of a coherent constitutional principle.

So, then, constitutional law is not made from sociology, and neither does a change in sociology affect the decision.

Social Science Data in Shaping the Remedy or Vindicating the Rights of the Aggrieved Party

Although social science evidence is not valuable in judging constitutional validity, it is useful once the principal decision has been made. Its value is in designing a remedy. Expert witnesses and consultants are essential at the remedy stage because the court without help is ill-equipped for the task of prescribing a plan for desegregation, requiring as it does decisions involving educational issues as well as sensitive policy questions, such as length of transportation, and also knowledge of the character of the school district. Dr. Jack Finger, for example, is a well-recognized expert consultant who has served in numerous instances. Persons of his caliber render invaluable aid to a trial court.

Since the court is placed in the position at this stage of a case of considering policy matters, it must seek out the best educational advice, data, and analysis that it can find.[25] In this connection, it is necessary to have social science research, educational research, and even engineering (the latter for a transportation plan). In addition, the court must seek out the views of the school district staff and seek a proposed plan from that organization, since it has the primary responsibility for coming up with a plan. In most cases, however, the final responsibility falls on the court. Frequently, the school district seeks to avoid participation in desegregation and integration orders from the standpoint of policy-making (and I cannot fault this too much).

Implementing and Executing

Once a decree is entered, the school district is faced with carrying out its terms so as to bring about a smooth transition. From that point the problem is *carrying out* the law.

Inservice Training for the Teachers and School Staff

One area in which social science assistance proves helpful is in a program to prepare teachers and principals for a desegregation effort. This preparation is of the very highest importance. An extensive and concentrated curriculum starting three or four months before the beginning of school and continuing for an equal length of time after school has started, giving inservice training to the teaching and administrative staff, is of primary importance and value. This preparation is designed to impress the school administrative and teaching staffs with the sensitive human relations problems presented and with the necessity for approaching the undertaking with apprehension but also enthusiasm, spirit, patience, understanding, and intelligence. The plan is going to stand or fall, in the final analysis, on the leadership at the school level. Experience has shown that the success of the program is in proportion to the ability and enthusiasm of the teachers and principals.[26]

The Language Problem—An Impediment to Equal Educational Opportunity

Frequently there is more than one minority group, and this poses a language problem.[27] Thus, in San Francisco there is a Chinese-speaking minority; in many of the western states, there is a Spanish-speaking minority. The Supreme Court in the *Keyes*[28] decision was of the opinion that there could be no distinction drawn between the black minority students and the Chicano students insofar as desegregation was concerned, but this ruling did not preclude giving special attention to the language problem. On this issue, the testimony presented on behalf of such a minority group focused on their special language needs, which are distinct from needs of the black community, for example.[29] Sometimes there is a complete inability to speak English and this, of course, calls for very special attention. To fail to do so creates a condition of terrible frustration for the students involved, but large numbers of Chicanos are inefficient in speaking English and need to develop proficiency if their education is going to be a successful experience. The court does not fully appreciate this unless expert testimony is presented. Certainly mere desegregation and integration orders cannot in these circumstances produce an atmosphere of learning that will fill the bill. The frustration of the Spanish-speaking student in being subjected to what has been called a cold turkey approach creates bad educational results, and although the object is to develop their language skills in English, the use of their native language may well prove to be extremely helpful.

The ruling of the Court of Appeals of the Tenth Circuit in *Keyes* was that the program prescribed was not justified on the basis of constitutional requirements.[30] At the same time, the court left open the prescribing of language education such as has been described above.

Monitoring and Supporting the Plan

Social science data and analysis provide backing for another aspect in the implementation of the decree. This was included in the Denver school desegregation plan. As part of the decree, a "Community Education Council" was set up with responsibility and authority to monitor the progress of desegregation in the schools and to report to the court. People representing a broad spectrum of community groups—racial, social, economic, religious—can be appointed to such a council in the hopes of mobilizing community support behind making the transition to desegregation effective and peaceful. The most important factor in such an effort is leadership. The council or monitoring group should be community leaders, and there should be an outstanding community leader as chairman. Chancellor Maurice Mitchell of the University of Denver, a distinguished educator, was and is the Chairman of the Denver Council, and he is indeed exemplary. This monitoring program has importance equal to that of the inservice program mentioned above in the ultimate success of a plan. Both play essential roles in supporting the program in terms of upholding the law and preventing possible disruption.[31]

Of great importance also is the participation of various community groups in the program. These include leaders of higher education institutions, business organizations, and such community groups as the League of Women Voters, Council of Jewish Women, the bar associations, medical associations, Junior League, the Chamber of Commerce, and the Junior Chamber of Commerce. The presence of such organizations furnishes a broad representation of the community; even though the members may not subscribe to all aspects of the effort, there is nevertheless a common bond that brings and holds these community groups together, and that is the necessity for upholding the Constitution and laws.

In the final analysis, then, social science confirms what our common sense tells us: desegregation alone is no quick solution to the educational problems of those whose constitutional rights were violated for so long. The real challenge is in the individual schools and the real holders of responsibility are individual principals and teachers, together with the community. But this is fitting in our constitutional democracy. The courts may well declare what the Constitution requires, but the test of our democratic system is whether each individual can come to see his responsibility to his fellow person and the law.

Finally, social evidence and data have their place in the economic case, Title VII, child labor, etc., but not in school desegregation. So if the foes of school cases feel that the problem will evaporate if social evidence is eliminated, they had better reassess their position.

Notes

[1]Now codified at 28 U.S.C. Section 1343.

[2]Now codified at 42 U.S.C. Section 200e *et seq.*

[3]*Adams v. Turner*, 244 U.S. 590, 600 (1917) (dissenting), quoted in A. Bickel, *The Supreme Court and the Idea of Progress* 21 (1970). See also *Burns Baking Co. v. Bryan*, 264 U.S. 504, 520 (1924) (Brandeis, J., dissenting): "Knowledge is essential to understanding, and understanding should precede judging." See generally, Social science research and the law: a symposium in honor of Hans Zeisel, 41 *University of Chicago Law Review* 209 (1974).

[4]See, *e.g., New State Ice Co. v. Liebman*, 285 U.S. 262 (1932); *Adkins v. Children's Hosp.*, 261 U.S. 525 (1923); *Coppage v. Kansas*, 236 U.S. 1 (1915); *Lochner v. New York*, 198 U.S. 45 (1905).

[5]See, *e.g., West Coast Hotel v. Parrish*, 300 U.S. 379 (1937); *Home Building & Loan Ass'n v. Blaisdell*, 290 U.S. 398 (1934); *Bunting v. Oregon*, 243 U.S. 426 (1917); cf. *Mugler v. Kansas*, 123 U.S. 623 (1887). See generally, Kohn, Social psychological data, legislative fact, and constitutional law, 29 *George Washington Law Review* 136 (1960).

[6]*Muller v. Oregon*, 208 U.S. 412 (1908) (Brief for the Defendant in Error, submitted by Louis Brandeis).

[7]Pound, The scope and purpose of sociological jurisprudence, 24 *Harvard Law Review* 591 (1911). See generally, Pound, 1 *Jurisprudence* Sections 22-29 (1959).

[8]Now codified at 15 U.S.C. Section 1.

[9]See *United States v. Topco Assoc. Inc.*, 405 U.S. 596 (1972); *Standard Oil Co. v. United States*, 221 U.S. 1 (1911).

[10]See, *e.g., United States v. General Dynamics Corp.*, 415 U.S. 486 (1974); *United States v. Columbia Steel*, 334 U.S. 495 (1948); *United States v. Socony-Vacuum Oil Co.*, 310 U.S. 510 (1940).

[11]*Williams v. Florida*, 399 U.S. 78 (1970).

[12]*Furman v. Georgia*, 408 U.S. 238 (1972).

[13]*Powell v. Texas*, 392 U.S. 514 (1968).

[14]*Robinson v. California*, 370 U.S. 660 (1962).

[15]*San Antonio Independent School District v. Rodriguez*, 411 U.S. 1 (1973).

[16]See *Smith v. California*, 361 U.S. 147, 160-161, 164-167, 171-172 (1959); cf. *Paris Adult Theatre I v. Slaton*, 413 U.S. 49, 56 n. 6 (1973).

[17]*McDonell Douglas v. Green*, 411 U.S. 792 (1973); *Griggs v. Duke Power*, 401 U.S. 424 (1971).

[18]347 U.S. 483 (1954).

[19]163 U.S. 537 (1896).

[20]See *Stell v. Chatham, Board of Education*, 333 F. 2d 55 (Fifth Circuit 1964), *rev'g* 220 F. Supp. 667 (S.D.Ga. 1963).

[21]*Keyes v. School District No. 1*, 413 U.S. 189 (1973). Thus, if a demographic study showed that, after residential population shifts by blacks, new school boundary lines were drawn that matched the areas of increased black population, that social science study would be important evidence. It may also be possible to demonstrate through social science data that a school violation in one district has had inter-district effects, or that state policies in areas such as housing and zoning have had the effect of segregating schools—with the result that an inter-district remedy may be appropriate. See *Milliken v. Bradley*, 418 U.S. 747 (1974); Pettigrew, A sociological view of the post-*Bradley* era, 21 *Wayne Law Review* 13 (1975); Taueber, Demographic perspectives on housing and school segregation, 21 *Wayne Law Review* 833 (1975).

[22]See 347 U.S. at 494 n. 11.

[23]We are mindful that the Court made a passing reference in footnote 11 to various scholarly data, but this was in support of the Court's conclusion that segregation engenders a feeling of inferiority in the child, which is in line with the supporting constitutional law reasons.

[24]J. Coleman, "Recent Trends in School Integration," paper presented to American Educational Research Association, April 2, 1975.

[25]See generally, Foster, Techniques of school desegregation, 44 *Harvard Educational Review* (1974); R. Crain and C. Rossell, "Evaluating School Desegregation Plans Statistically" (1973).

[26]See, *e.g.*, Orfield, How to make desegregation work: the adaptation of schools to their newly-integrated student bodies, 39 *Law and Contemporary Problems* 314 (1975); Hawley and Rist, On the future implementation of school desegregation: some considerations, 39 *Law and Contemporary Problems* 412 (1975). See also Weinberg, The relationship between school desegregation and academic achievement: a review of the research, 39 *Law and Contemporary Problems* 241; 1-2 National Opinion Research Center, "Southern Schools: An Evaluation of the Effects of the Emergency School Assistance Program and of School Desegregation" (1973). The impression one gets from this literature is that the success of desegregation—even if measured by such education outputs as achievement scores—turns more on how desegregation is accomplished in a particular school district—how particular principals and teaching staffs react—than on any magic percentage mixture of minorities and Anglos.

[27]See, *e.g.*, Levin and Moise, School desegregation litigation in the 1970's and the use of social science evidence: an annotated guide, 39 *Law and Contemporary Problems* 50, 74-80, 114-120 (1975); United States Commission on Civil Rights, "Mexican-American Education Study: Report VI, Toward Quality Education for Mexican-Americans" (1974); Grubb, Breaking the language barrier: the right to bilingual education, 9 *Harvard Civil Rights-Civil Liberties Law Review* 52 (1974).

[28]413 U.S. 189 (1973).

[29]*Keyes v. School District No. 1*, 380 F. Supp. 673 (D. Colo. 1974).

[30]*Keyes v. School District No. 1*, 521 F. 2d 465 (Tenth Circuit 1975).

[31]See note 26, *supra*.

Social Sciences and Constitutional Rights– The Consequences of Uncertainty

Ronald Dworkin

One question is central to the issue raised by the interrelationship of education, social science, and the judicial process. Certain decisions by the federal courts, including the Supreme Court, require positive steps to be taken toward school integration, using strategies that include busing. There is a widespread belief that these decisions rest on certain propositions that may either be confirmed or disconfirmed by what is called the social sciences. The problem is this: these various propositions now appear to be more doubtful than they were several years ago. This doubt raises two questions. The first is, does this suggest that the judicial decisions were in fact wrong? Must any doubt we might have about these propositions of social science be translated into doubts about the soundness of the decisions that ordered integration? The second question, dependent on the first, is this: suppose we decided that that *is* so. The doubts about these propositions must be translated into doubts about the decisions. Can we, or should we, draw any general lesson about the use of such propositions in the adjudicative process generally? Should we conclude that, if we have gotten our hands burnt in using social science in adjudication, then we ought to stay away from that kind of fire in the future? These seem to be the two questions central to this collection of essays.

But I want to begin by urging upon you a distinction. It might be a mistake, and it might indeed retard our analysis, if we continue to assume that there is some methodological technique that is practiced in common between, let us say, economics on the one hand and anthropology or history on the other. Much has been written about the philosophy of the social sciences, and I am not going to summarize even a corner of the literature;

but I do wish to call to your attention a distinction frequently made in that literature. This is the distinction between two kinds of judgments or hypotheses, both of which belong to the social sciences in the sense that they are made by people who profess to be members of some discipline called a social science. Causal judgments are judgments that assert a causal connection between two independently specifiable social phenomena. A very good example can be drawn from economics: An economist says "Allowing unemployment to rise will decrease the rate of inflation." This is a prediction that assumes a causal connection between two phenomena—the rate of unemployment and the rate of inflation. An interpretative judgment, on the other hand, does not, at least on the surface, assert a causal relationship between two independent and specifiable phenomena, but rather locates a particular phenomenon within a particular category of phenomena by specifying its meaning within the society in which it occurs. The judgment of an anthropologist who says that a particular practice—say a rain dance in some primitive tribe—is religious rather than technological in its meaning is not a causal judgment. Frazer, who wrote the famous book *The Golden Bough*, observed that certain people in the South Seas had very poor technology—they were a rather stupid people—because they danced to cause it to rain, and this was very bad agricultural practice. In fact, Frazer had made a mistake of interpretative judgment because, as later anthropologists pointed out, it was wrong to regard what they were doing as technological and therefore to be understood as somehow resting on their assumptions about causal connections. It was rather part of religion and had to be interpreted using their concepts that way.

It would be wrong to insist on too fine a distinction between causal and interpretative judgments. Causal judgments have interpretative elements, because they must classify the phenomena between which they assert a causal connection. Interpretative judgments have a causal background, because the idea of meaning in social science cannot be explicated fully without causal ideas. But we can nevertheless make the distinction sufficiently clearly for present purposes by supposing that the interpretative elements in causal judgments, and the causal elements in interpretative judgments, are matters of background, not part of the point of the judgment.

The distinction is relevant to our discussion because two kinds of judgments, one causal and one interpretative, have been thought by many people to be the foundation upon which different decisions in the chain of decisions from *Brown* to *Milliken v. Bradley* rest. There are a variety of plainly causal hypotheses that are supposed to be necessary predicates for the later decisions, those that required state agencies affirmatively to integrate schools. I shall mention these, although I am sure I will do it badly and crudely. There is first the harm hypothesis, which roughly speaking states that segregated education is poor education, that is, that segregated education harms the educational opportunity of those, particularly members of minority groups, who are subjected to it. There is, second, what I shall call the consequential hypothesis. This supposes that *de facto* segregation is the consequence, or at least may fairly be presumed to be the consequence, of earlier *de jure* segregation. There is, third, what I shall call the efficacy hypothesis, which argues that techniques like busing do more good than harm, that is, that they achieve something that we as a society do or ought to value more than we value what is lost through these techniques in resentment and amenity.

There are three causal hypotheses. They are thought to be necessary to justify at least certain of the judicial decisions that require integration, or at least, certain of the practices. Although I understood Judge Doyle to dissent from that judgment, most of his colleagues, and most academic lawyers, seem to accept it.[1]

It is, however, widely thought that the original decision in *Brown* and the decisions immediately following *Brown*, which dealt with *de jure* segregation, do not rest upon those three causal judgments at all, but instead may be sufficiently justified by an interpretative judgment of social science, namely the judgment that segregation is degrading or insulting to the black minority.

Professor Clark mentioned Cahn's essay written just after the *Brown* decision in which he said that he would hate to think that constitutional rights rest on judgments of social science. He meant to say, I think, that these early decisions did not rest on *causal* judgments, because he went on to justify *Brown* by invoking an *interpretative* judgment of social science—the one I just mentioned, that is, that segregation is, in and of itself, insulting and degrading. I think it wrong to suggest that Cahn thought this was a value judgment *as distinct from* a judgment of social science. What I recall is that he said something like this: "We don't need evidence for the proposition that segregation is an insult to the black community—we *know* it." If I remember rightly he said—"We know it the way we know that a cold causes sniffles." It isn't that we don't *need* to know it, it isn't that there isn't something there to know. There is a fact of the matter, namely that segregation is an insult, but we don't need evidence for that fact—we just know it. It is an interpretative fact.

I emphasize the importance of this distinction for two reasons. First, it seems to me possible that we underplay the extent to which the later decisions, the decisions affirmatively requiring integration, might also be shown to rest upon interpretative rather than causal judgments of social science. Second, if we ask whether it is appropriate for the judiciary to look to judgments of social science, we will get very different answers to the question depending upon whether we have causal judgments or interpretative judgments in mind.

I shall start with the latter of those two suggestions. Social scientists argue for causal judgments, like the harm hypothesis, the consequence hypothesis, and the efficacy hypothesis, through statistical correlations rather than by producing any mechanical model that would teach us the way in which, or describe the technique through which, the cause produces the effect. It is quite typical, of course, in social science that they must do this. In physics, it is now thought to be an unsound judgment that rests merely on correlation between observable events unsupported by some notion of the mechanics that translate the cause to the effect. In social science, we do not have, or we have only to an extremely sketchy degree, the mechanics; we simply have the correlation. Sometimes, of course, we must act on what we have. The hypothesis that smoking cigarettes causes cancer is still largely at the stage of correlation. We still lack, so far as I know, anything persuasive by way of a story of *how* smoking produces the disease.

When judgments rest simply on correlations between observed phenomena, there is necessarily an element of arbitrariness introduced by the choice of categories whose correlation is taken to be significant. Several of the other contributors to this volume state that they feel the arbitrariness of social scientific conclusions about race and harm. The choice here is not restricted, as it is in physical science, by the requirements of a dominant mechanical model, or by the requirement to provide a substitute for the dominant model. That is a substantial difference between social science and the physical sciences that we must always bear in mind. It has a further consequence. When you lack a mechanical model, and you make judgments simply on correlations between observed phenomena, the kinds of techniques necessary to provide arguments for and against the hypothesis belong entirely to a very arcane subject, namely, statistics. The mathematical concepts of statistics are much more removed from the ordinary vocabulary of a trial judge than are the concepts of physics or chemistry that he might encounter in, for example, a complicated patent case. This accounts, I think, to a large degree, for the sense of distance and dependence a judge has when asked to consider complex causal hypotheses in social science.

There is one further point. Correlations of social phenomena are fragile in the sense that the data, the behavior that forms the correlation, can change very quickly. Furthermore, the fact of an hypothesis—the fact that a correlation has been made—can affect this change. This is what is called the Heisenberg effect.

We find, in these considerations, ample reason to deplore any general dependence of adjudication on complex judgments of causal social science, particularly when constitutional rights are at stake. But these objections do not apply to interpretative judgments, like the judgment that a particular practice is insulting or is seen by the community as a religious ritual rather than a technological effort. Interpretative judgments are different because they must be framed in the critical vocabulary of the community in question, and that requirement, although not the same as the requirement of a mechanical model, provides the same kind of anchor, the same refuge from the arbitrary. Interpretative judgments are also much more enduring because they are based on judgments of convention, that is, of shared understandings that reinforce each other and cannot change in the way in which independently described behavior, of the sort that figures in statistical correlations, can change. But the most important difference is this: Interpretative judgments are not foreign to the judge; they do not draw on a kind of technology that is for him arcane. On the contrary, they draw upon the same kinds of skills, and are indeed identical in their structure, with the judgment that a judge makes when he draws from a line of precedent a characterization that seems to him a more sensitive characterization of the precedents than any other. In other words, interpretative judgments study society and its practices in the same way that ordinary judgments of adjudication—the kind of judgments judges make in hard cases all the time—study standard legal materials.[2]

This distinction, then—between causal and interpretative judgments—gives us a kind of functional analysis of why the causal judgments of social science cause trouble in the judicial process, but why interpretative judgments are native to that process. I now want to return to the first suggestion I made. Must we really say, looking back on the later decisions—those that require affirmative action to eradicate *de facto* segregation—that these later decisions rest on causal judgments, so that if we are suspicious of causal judgments then we must be suspicious of these decisions? That is a very difficult question. It requires an exercise in that border area between law and philosophy that I think is typical of legal analysis. Let us spread out these decisions: the *Swann* case, *Keyes*, *Milliken*, and the rest. Let us spread them out and take from them crudely a series of propositions of law, like the proposition that *de jure* segregation is illegal in itself; that when *de facto* segregation can be shown to have followed *de jure* segregation, then integrating remedies are appropriate; and so forth.

Let us ask this question: what political theory can we describe such that, if we accepted that political theory, these cases would therefore be justified as a matter of political morality? What do we have to assume about political rights, political goals, political morality—what do we have to assume in order to suppose that these decisions are right as a matter of political principle? I am not quite asking the question "what political theory can we draw from the Constitution that would support these decisions?" We will ultimately, as lawyers wish to ask that question, but I am asking a more fundamental question first.

We might make a start on that fundamental question this way. Suppose we assume that the various judgments of causal social sciences I mentioned—the hypotheses of harm, efficacy, and consequence—are sound as a matter of social science. Suppose we assume for the moment that they are right. Can we find in political morality a theory that, assuming their soundness, would justify these decisions? If not, then the decisions do not rest on the assumptions that the hypotheses are sound; and so they are not called into question when the hypotheses are doubted.

There are two apparent possibilities; two possible arguments that might be thought to justify these decisions if the causal hypotheses of harm, consequence, or efficacy are sound. The first theory argues that an integrated education is a *right*, an individual right, that every child has, or every child born into a minority has, presumably protected by the Constitution but in any case protected by political morality. The second theory argues not that integration is a right but that integration is a *remedy;* it is the appropriate remedy for past injustice. Each of these theories fails, even if we assume that the causal hypotheses upon which it is based are sound. There is a third possible theory: it denies that integration is a right, denies that integration is justified as a remedy, but argues that integration is a commanding social goal, so that the states have affirmative responsibility to reach integration on that ground. The third theory fails also, but since I have never heard it proposed, I shall not consider it here. But I wish to show you the reasons I have for thinking that these theories fail.

Consider the first theory, that integration is a right. Note two preliminary points. First, the idea that integration is a constitutionally protected right, or a right protected by political morality, does indeed require us to accept the causal hypothesis that I called the hypothesis of harm. The syllogism appears to be this. Every child is entitled to an equal educational opportunity. A segregated education, whether *de jure* or *de facto*, does not provide an equal educational opportunity. Therefore every child is entitled to an integrated education. Secondly, if we wish to adopt this theory as a justification of the integration cases, then we must ignore a part of the opinion in each case, namely, the part of the opinion that appears to say that no remedy exists for *de facto* segregation unless the district has been segregated *de jure,* covertly or openly, in the past. If every child has a right to an integrated education, then it cannot make any difference whether a *de facto* segregated district was segregated *de jure* in the past. However, it was widely thought, before *Milliken v. Bradley,* that the requirement of past *de jure* segregation was so much window dressing, because the courts would, in effect, infer past *de jure* from present *de facto* segregation in every case. Professor Owen Fiss makes that point.[3] So we might well be willing, for purposes of the argument, both to accept the hypothesis of harm and to ignore the language in the opinions that appears troublesome.

Does the assumption of a right to an integrated education then justify the decisions? No, for the following reasons. The causal hypothesis of harm is statistical in two ways. It is not only statistical in the sense that I mentioned before, that is, that it rests on statistical correlations. It is also statistical in the different sense that, even if it is true, it can be true only for the bulk of the members of any given minority. There will be some members of that minority who will have a worse education in an integrated school than in a segregated school. People just do differ to that extent. Now, if the syllogism on which the theory of rights depends were sound, then some such child, whoever he or she is, can deploy that syllogism before us with equal rigor but to the opposite effect. He can say: "For me, an integrated education does not provide the level of educational opportunity to which I am entitled. Therefore, I am entitled to a segregated education." We cannot, it seems to me, use numbers to adjudicate rights. So the fact that the judgment goes through for him, to a different conclusion, is an effective answer to the claim that people have by virtue of a general right to an equal educational opportunity a special right to a particular facility that will provide that education only for some of them.

Let me, therefore, consider the second theory, which is that integration is justified, not because everybody has a right to integration, but because integration is the appropriate remedy for the past injustice of *de jure* segregation. This theory does not suffer from the difficulties of the theory that integration is a right in itself. It is not vulnerable, in the first place, to the point just made against that theory. It provides an answer of a kind to the child who says that he will be harmed by integration, which is this: "We are *not* assuming that every child has a right to that form of education that works best for him. Therefore you cannot complain that we must respect *your* right to that form of education that works best for you. But for a past injustice, the *de jure* segregation, you would be having an integrated education now. Although you may prefer a segregated education for one reason or another, you are not entitled to retain the benefit of someone's past injustice."

Nor does the second theory require that we ignore those parts of the earlier opinions that said that remedies against *de facto* segregation were only available if there had been a background of *de jure* segregation. On the contrary, it requires that we pay very strict attention to that requirement instead of dismissing it as window dressing, as we just did.

The second theory does, however, require us to accept the consequence hypothesis, and not only to accept it but to embrace it in an extraordinarily strong form. Let us now distinguish two versions of the consequence hypothesis. There is a weak version, which says that if there was *de jure* segregation in the past then that *de jure* segregation may be presumed to be part of the causal chain that has produced (perhaps through affecting residential patterns, perhaps in other ways) *de facto* segregation of today. Many of us would find that weak judgment plausible. The strong consequence hypothesis requires that we accept much more than that. It requires us to accept that, if there had not been *de jure* segregation in the past, there would now be *de facto* integration. The first, the weak consequence hypothesis, merely supposes that *de jure* segregation figured in the chain of events that actually produced the present situation. The second says that *de jure* segregation is a necessary pre-condition of *de facto* segregation. It denies the possibility (or at least it says that it is extremely improbable) that if there had never been *de jure* segregation, *de facto* segregation would have come about in some other way.

If the second theory tells the student whose education will be harmed by integration that he would no doubt have suffered that harm if there were no past injustice, then it relies on the strong form of the consequence hypothesis. I know of no evidence that is even putatively enough to support such a strong assumption. But since we are attempting to see whether any causal hypothesis figures in the justification of the later judicial decisions, let us *assume* that the strong consequentialist hypothesis—that earlier *de jure* segregation is a necessary condition for *de facto* segregation—is true.

What then? The second theory still fails. Consider the position of some child (perhaps a white child) whose education will suffer if busing is ordered, *not* because an integrated education will in itself be any worse for him, but because of the dislocations and inefficiencies and antagonisms that busing will produce. We may say that if there had been no *de jure* segregation, he would have had an integrated education. That follows from the strong form of the consequence hypothesis, which we are supposing is true. But we cannot say that busing will restore him to the position he would have occupied had there been no prior injustice. In that event he would have attended an integrated neighborhood school set in an integrated neighborhood, without social tensions. We have produced instead a new situation that is, by hypothesis, much worse, and where his educational opportunities will be more limited. It cannot be said, in rebuttal, that he has in some way benefited by the past injustice and therefore it is fair that he should now suffer. He is not guilty of any wrong. Nor (again by hypothesis) has he gained through the wrong of another. There is no unjust enrichment at all.

Where do we stand? I've argued that, if we look for a philosophically satisfying rationale for the later desegration decisions, then the two theories that might seem initially the most plausible, but which rest on causal hypotheses, must be disqualified even if we accept these causal hypotheses as true. I now wish to sketch for you (and even "sketch" might be too arrogant a word) a different justification for these decisions, a justification that rests on interpretative rather than on causal judgments.

We must begin at the beginning. The right to equality embedded in the equal protection clause cannot be understood without the following distinctions. There are two distinct rights that might be subsumed under that clause. The first is the right to equal treatment over a certain range of goods, of which education might be one—equal treatment, such that each person gets the same as the next. That cannot be the *general* rationale of the equal protection clause because, although the right to equal treatment holds with respect to some goods (like voting power), it does not hold for all. Otherwise the government could never discriminate in the general interest. The second is the right, not to equal treatment, but to treatment as an equal. And that right is at the heart of the equal protection clause.

But it is very hard to say what the right to treatment as an equal requires in practice. I argue that it means that government making political decisions must treat each individual, as an individual, with equal concern and respect. That means that any political judgment about what makes the community better as a whole must count the impact on each particular person as having the same importance. As Bentham said, "Each man [he should have added "and woman"] to count for one and none for more than one."

The political process in a democracy is meant to translate that requirement into legislation through the institutions of representative democracy. The welfare economists have worked out a theory, which I call "preference utilitarianism," as to how that is achieved. Each individual, through his votes and other political activity, registers or reveals a preference. The political process is a machine that is calculated, although imperfectly, to reach decisions such that, although some individuals suffer and others gain, the *overall* preferences of all the people, considered neutrally with the same consideration for the preferences of each, are improved.

In a community that has settled prejudice of one sort or another, however, whether it be prejudice against blacks or against homosexuals or against particular political views, the machine will inevitably break down because there is no way of excluding these preferences based on prejudice from affecting the process. If prejudicial preferences are counted, then the personal preferences of those against whom the prejudice is directed are not counted equally in the balance; they are discounted by the effect of the prejudice. Therefore we need constitutional rights.

A constitutional right is created among other reasons for this reason:

We know that there is a high antecedent probability that the political judgment reached about a particular matter will not fairly reflect the kind of preferences that rightly make up the general welfare, but will give influential expression to preferences based on prejudice. We create constitutional rights of one sort or another to guard against this.

The key point of this explanation of constitutional rights is that rights are based on antecedent probabilities. We cannot say, for certain, that a particular law restricting speech, for example, is the result of prejudice against the view being expressed rather than the result of the fact that voters do not like noise. We have a sense, based on our knowledge of our own community, and a more general sense of human nature, that certain kinds of political decision have so high an antecedent probability of corruption that we cannot trust the political powers to make those decisions.

Certain of these kinds of decisions are specifically identified by substantive constitutional provisions like the First Amendment. But the equal protection clause simply provides that *no* decisions with a high antecedent probability of corruption through prejudice should be left to the normal political process.

That is the meaning of the idea of "suspect classifications" that now dominates equal protection theory. But the choice of these suspect classifications is a matter of interpretation. It is a matter of understanding the meaning of a pattern of preferences within the community. We know that *de jure* segregation is an insult, rather than the product of equal concern, in the same way that we know that a rain dance is religious and not technological, although we have more confidence in the former than in the latter judgment, because the community it judges is our own.

Consider now the case of political decisions assigning children to schools by drawing district lines. Suppose that the natural way of drawing district lines produces segregated schools because neighborhoods are segregated. The community is faced with a political decision. Would it be in the general interest to adopt extraordinary methods, like busing, to achieve integration? Or would the objective costs of that decision outweigh the gains? There is a high antecedent probability that any community decisions on that issue will be corrupted, high enough, since the matter is plainly important, to call for constitutional interventions. But what remedy is available as the vehicle of that intervention?

In the case of free speech, the vehicle of constitutional intervention is apparent. We provide a constitutional right guaranteeing the liberty to speak if you want. But the matter cannot be that simple in the case of school assignment. Why? Because we cannot create a comparable discretionary right—that is, a right an individual can exercise or not. A school district cannot provide a school of one's choice; it provides a school. And therefore the normal strategy of a discretionary right, like the right to speak or not, or to have an abortion or not, will not work. The special features of the school assignment issue therefore require different kinds of rights.

But what *kind* of rights? We might well approach that question backwards. Under what circumstances, different from the present, would we be willing to say that a particular decision on pupil assignment was *not* corrupt, and so could stand without interference from the judiciary? There are two possibilities. First, we might relax our judgment that such decisions are antecedently likely to be corrupt. We would do this on the basis of an interpretative judgment that society had changed. The background of preferences, beliefs, ideologies—in short, the background of prejudice—could have lifted, as we all hope some day it will. The background could change in another way. Members of the minority who are supposedly disadvantaged may assume political power to such a degree, at least power over school assignment decisions, that we need no longer worry about the antecedent probability that these decisions are corrupted by prejudice against them.

Suppose, however, that the background has not changed—prejudice has not lessened much and blacks do not have the kind of political power that would cancel any antecedent probability of corruption. What else would persuade us to disregard that probability in any particular case? Only one thing: the outcome. If the decision actually produced by the political process was of a sort *itself* to negate the change of corruption, then we could withdraw, for that case, the judgment that the process was too corrupt to allow it to continue.

We must understand a court order to integrate, even an order based upon a mechanical formula that otherwise has no appeal, in the following way. The order speaks to those in political power and says this: "If you refuse yourself to produce an outcome that negates the antecedent probability of corruption, then we must impose upon you such an outcome. The only decision that we can impose, given the nature of the problem, is a decision that requires integration on some formula that is evidently not corrupt even if it is just as evidently arbitrary."

If I am right, then objections to these decisions based on doubt about the various causal hypotheses I identified are misguided, because these decisions do not rest on causal hypotheses. They rest on interpretative theory. Until the background changes in one of the two ways I suggested—until our sense of prejudice abates or blacks have the political power to make decisions in question—until that happens, then integration is required as the only thing that can sustain the burden of proof rising from the antecedent probability of corruption.

I cannot now consider the second question I raised several pages ago, the general question of whether judgments of social science have a place in constitutional adjudication. I hope that what I think is apparent in what I have said about the integration cases. I said that controversial causal judgments based on statistical theory lie outside the normal competence of courts, because these judgments are anchored in any model that contains their arbitrary and transient character. I am therefore sympathetic to doubts that these judgments should be given great weight. But I am hostile to any attempts to reduce the role of interpretative judgments. The judicial process must inevitably give large place to interpretative judgments. Indeed, if the analysis I sketched is right, then interpretative judgments are at the center of every decision involving the equal protection clause. They can be driven from constitutional decisions only at the cost of driving that clause from the Constitution.

Notes

[1]*Cf.* William E. Doyle, Social science evidence in court cases, *supra.*

[2]I have defended that claim at some length in an article called Hard cases, 88 *Harvard Law Review* 1057 (1975).

[3]*Cf.* Owen Fiss, The jurisprudence of busing, 34 *Law and Contemporary Problems* 194 (1975).

Implementing the Promise of <u>Brown</u>: Social Science and the Courts in Future School Litigation

Julius L. Chambers

References in *Brown v. Board of Education*[1] to various social science data that supported the opinion have provided opportunities for extended criticisms of the basic holding[2] and of judicial remedies for implementation.[3] Analyses of the social science data and of subsequent studies and events have lead some to suggest that *Brown* should be reversed[4] or that alternative remedies to desegregation should be considered.[5] The papers in this volume focus on some of these criticisms and the use of social science by the judiciary in educational problem solving.

This paper advances the proposition that the emphasis on social science data in school desegregation litigation is misplaced; that the supporting basis for *Brown* was the equal protection clause; and that the use of social science in future school litigation should focus on how to improve desegregated educational programs rather than on how to devise alternative remedies.

I

For those committed to desegregated education, the necessity for a conference in 1976 to review and analyze the judicial approach to educational problem solving and implementation of *Brown* must cause some concern. More than twenty years after *Brown*, after agonizing and frustrating efforts[6] and with many school districts as segregated as they were before 1954,[7] we are still considering judicial alternatives to desegregation. Many members of Congress and the executive branch have for all intents and purposes abandoned the effort.[8] Recent decisions[9] of the Courts raise grave doubts as to the continued commitment of the judiciary to school desegregation. The extended controversy gives some credence to the earlier prophesy of Professor Bickel[10] that sustained and widely-accepted objections to *Brown* may eventually lead to its rejection.

Much of today's criticisms of *Brown* and implementing decisions result from earlier and present assertions that the supporting basis for the decisions was the social science studies that indicated that compulsory segregation produced an insurmountable inferiority complex in black children and deprived them of an equal opportunity to achieve educationally.[11] It was not the social science data, however, but the equal protection clause that warranted the determination that separate and equal educational facilities should not be condoned.[12] In order to appreciate this determination by the Court, it is important to go back and review the legal rights accorded to blacks immediately preceding and following the Emancipation Proclamation.

Prior to 1862, because slavery was valid in some states and invalid in others, the issue arose in *Dred Scott v. Sandford*,[13] regarding the status of black persons as they moved from one geographic location to another. Did the right of property in a black person born a slave in one state re-attach when the person returned from a free state with the consent of his owner? State courts treating the issue reached conflicting conclusions and the federal law remained unsettled. Dred Scott, a former slave in Missouri, was removed to a free territory by his owner and subsequently returned to the State of Missouri voluntarily. Scott alleged that the owner Sandford owed him monetary damages for battery and false imprisonment upon his return. Sandford admitted that he had laid his hands upon Scott and imprisoned him, but asserted that this was no more than he might lawfully do if Scott were a slave. The lower court held that Scott as a descendant of slaves was not a citizen, and, therefore, could not seek relief in Federal Courts. It was further argued that he remained a slave despite his departure to and from free territory. On review by the United States Supreme Court, the lower court's decision was upheld. In writing for the Court, Mr. Justice Taney went further and declared that the entire Negro race was excluded from citizenship. In so ruling, he placed the official stamp of the Supreme Court on a theory of racial inferiority and degradation. Said the Court:

> The question is simply this: Can a Negro, whose ancestors were imported into this country, and sold as slaves, become a member of the political community formed and brought into existence by the Constitution of the United States, and as such become entitled to all the rights, and privileges, and immunities, guaranteed by that instrument to the citizen. . . . We think they are not. . . . On the contrary, they were at that time considered as a subordinate and inferior class of being, who had been subjugated by the

dominant race, and whether emancipated or not, yet remained subject to their authority, and had no rights or privileges but such as those who held the power and the government might choose to grant them. . . .

The legislation of the States . . . shows . . . the inferior and subject condition of that race at the time the Constitution was adopted, and long afterward. . . . [I]t is hardly consistent with the respect due to these States, to suppose that they regarded at that time, as fellow citizens and members of the sovereignty, a class of beings who they had thus stigmatized, and upon whom they had impressed such deep and enduring marks of inferiority and degradation. . . .

No one, we presume, supposes that any change in public opinion or feeling in relocation to this unfortunate race, in the civilized nations of Europe or in this country, should induce the Court to give the words of the Constitution a more liberal construction in their favor than they were intended to bear when the instrument was framed and adopted. . . . This Court was not created by the Constitution for such purposes. Higher and graver trusts have been confided to it and it must not falter in the path of duty.[14]

One of the central points of the *Dred Scott* decision was overruled in 1868 with the adoption of the Fourteenth Amendment to the Constitution.[15] The language in *Dred Scott* approving continued subjugation of blacks by the dominant race regardless of their legal status was never implicitly or explicitly overturned.

Slavery as an institution was, of course, abolished by the Emancipation Proclamation in 1862, and passage thereafter of the Thirteenth Amendment.[16] The abolition of slavery, however, had little effect on formal and informal segregation of the races practiced North and South. Some years prior to the emancipation, and eighteen years before the Fourteenth Amendment was passed, Boston, Massachusetts—like its sister cities in the South—separated children in public schools on the basis of race. In a legal challenge to the statute calling for such separation, plaintiffs argued that racial segregation inflicted upon black children the stigma of caste, subjected them to inconveniences in travel to which white children were not subjected, and gave them an inferior educational opportunity because "a school exclusively devoted to one class must differ essentially in its spirit and character, from that public school known to the law where all classes meet together in equality." The Court rejected these arguments on the basis that the lawmakers had grounds of reason and experience for requiring the segregation of schools.[17] The schools, although separate for the races, thus met the constitutional requirement of equality:

. . . The Committee, apparently upon great deliberation, have come to the conclusion, that the good of both classes of schools will be best promoted, by maintaining the separate primary schools for colored and white children, and we can perceive no ground to doubt, that this is the honest result of their experience and judgment.

It is urged that this maintenance of separate schools tends to deepen and perpetuate the odious distinction of caste, founded in a deep-rooted prejudice in public opinion. . . . [I]t is a fair and proper question for the committee to consider and decide upon, having in view the best interests of both classes of children placed under their superintendent, and we cannot say, that their decision upon it is not founded on just grounds of reason and experience, and the results of a discriminating and honest judgment.[18]

No effort was made by the Court to clarify what the "grounds of reason and experience" were, or to weigh those factors against the asserted harm. It did state, however, that "prejudice, if it exists, is not created by law, and probably cannot be changed by law."

In the South following emancipation, various "Black Codes" were adopted, which imposed every variety of legal disability on blacks. The Reconstruction Congress of 1866 passed The Civil Rights Act of 1866 designed to abolish these disabilities, guaranteeing to blacks born in the States citizenship, and the right to enter into all legal relations and to have equal benefits of all the laws as enjoyed by whites. The Fourteenth Amendment was passed in 1868, in part to provide Congress with constitutional power to enact legislation such as the Civil Rights Act of 1866. The Fifteenth Amendment was adopted shortly thereafter in 1870, and forbade a State to deny or abridge the right to vote "on account of race, color or previous condition of servitude."

In 1883, seventeen years after the Fourteenth Amendment had been passed to assure equality of blacks before the law, the United States Supreme Court in the *Civil Rights Cases*[19] invalidated a recently passed Civil Rights Act that would have guaranteed access to all public accommodations regardless of race on the basis of the equal protection clause of the Fourteenth Amendment. The Court held that this was a matter properly treated by the State, not the Federal, government. Viewing reconstruction as an era in which blacks were "special favorites of the law," the Court declared that the nation should return to legal neutrality on the subject of black rights:

When a man has emerged from slavery, and by the aid of beneficent legislation has shaken off the inseparable concomitants of that state, there must be some stage in the progress of his elevation when he takes the rank of a mere citizen, and ceases to be the special favorite of the laws, and when his rights, as a citizen or a man, are to be protected in the ordinary modes by which other men's rights are protected.[20]

There followed a pervasive range of official and unofficial means of maintaining racial segregation. Racial segregation of railroad passengers was a measure widely adopted. *Plessy v. Ferguson*[21] was the first case to reach the Supreme Court to test the validity of state-imposed segregation on railroad cars. In that decision, the majority of the Court upheld the Louisiana statute because it found the regulation to be reasonable:

> [T]he case reduces itself to the question whether the statute of Louisiana is a reasonable regulation, and with respect to this there must necessarily be a large discretion on the part of the legislature. In determining the question of reasonableness it is at liberty to act with reference to the established usages, customs and traditions of the people, and with a view to the promotion of their comfort, and the preservation of the public peace and good order. Gauged by this standard, we cannot say that a law which . . . requires the separation of the two races in public conveyances is unreasonable.[22]

Plaintiff's argument that such forced separation was a badge or incident of slavery and inferiority was rejected, the Court stating:

> We considered the underlying fallacy of the plaintiff's argument to consist in the assumption that the enforced separation of the two races stamps the colored race with a badge of inferiority. If this be so, it is not by reason of anything found in the Act, but solely because the colored race chooses to put that construction upon it.[23]

Mr. Justice Harlan, in a ringing dissent, condemned the argument for separate but equal facilities for the races in these terms:

> It was said in argument that the statute of Louisiana does not discriminate against either race, but prescribes a rule applicable alike to white and colored citizens. But this argument does not meet the difficulty. Everyone knows that the statute in question had its origin in the purpose, not so much to exclude white persons from railroad cars occupied by blacks, as to exclude colored people from coaches occupied by or assigned to white persons. . . . The thing to accomplish was, under the guise of giving equal accommodation for whites and blacks to compel the latter to keep to themselves while traveling in railroad passenger coaches. No one would be so wanting in candor as to assert the contrary. The fundamental objection, therefore, to the statute, is that it interferes with the personal freedom of citizens. . . .
>
> Sixty millions of whites are in no danger from the presence here of eight millions of blacks. The destinies of the two races in this country are indissolubly linked together, and the interests of both require that the common government of all shall not permit the seeds of race hate to be planted under the sanction of law. What can more certainly arouse race hate, what more certainly creates and perpetuates a feeling of distrust between these races, than state enactments which in fact proceed on the ground that colored citizens are so inferior and degraded that they cannot

be allowed to sit in public coaches occupied by white citizens? That, as all will admit, is the real meaning of such legislation as was enacted in Louisiana.[24]

The majority opinion in *Plessy* was a catalyst for further separation of the races in every sphere of social intercourse. Segregation in schools had, of course, existed prior to issuance of that opinion, but legal challenges to state bodies for failure to provide adequate educational opportunity to black citizens were after 1875 decided along the lines announced in *Plessy*. Thus, in *Cumming v. Richmond County Board of Education*,[25] just three years after *Plessy*, the Court sustained the authority of a school board to temporarily close a black high school while continuing to operate its white counterpart due to fiscal strain, since closing the white school would merely harm white students without providing additional educational opportunities for blacks. Deferring again to the power of the state to decide its own internal affairs, the Court stated:

> We may add that while all admit that the benefits and burdens of public taxation must be shared by citizens without discrimination against any class on account of their race, the education of the people in schools maintained by state taxation is a matter belonging to the respective states and any interference on the part of federal authorities with the management of such schools cannot be justified except in the case of a clear and unmistakable disregard of rights secured by the supreme law of the land. We have here no such state to be determined.[26]

The Supreme Court first reached the merits of the separate but equal doctrine in school segregation in a case involving a Chinese student excluded from white schools in Mississippi. The Court upheld her assignment to a black school, citing as authority *Roberts v. City of Boston*[27] and *Plessy v. Ferguson*.[28] *Roberts* was decided before the Fourteenth Amendment was enacted, and *Plessy* had, of course, concerned railroad cars. The Court thus declined to reach the issue of the legality of separation by full explanation of the constitutional issues on the ground that these issues had already been decided.

Some progress was made nonetheless at the insistence of black plaintiffs who began systematically to challenge the education afforded blacks by state agencies on grounds of their gross inequalities. In *Missouri ex rel Gaines v. Canada*,[29] the Supreme Court took the first important step in establishing minimum content for equality. There a black prospective law student was excluded from the only (white) law school in the State of Missouri but was eligible for payment from state funds of tuition fees to attend black law schools in neighboring states. The Court held that provision of tuition fees for out-of-state education for blacks was not sufficient to meet the requirements of substantial equality; black students could not constitutionally be put to the burden of having to leave the state to attend law school.

Similarly, in *Sipuel v. University of Oklahoma*,[30] a black applicant to the University of Oklahoma Law School was denied admission on the basis of race. Reversing the highest state court in Oklahoma (which had affirmed a lower court's denial of relief on grounds that the applicant should have elected out-of-state aid or demanded that a new institution be constructed for black citizens), the Court declared that the petitioner was entitled to secure the legal education afforded by the the state institution and to be provided that opportunity as soon as it was available to applicants of any other group.

Questions of where and when education was to be provided blacks were followed by consideration of how it was to be provided.[31] By 1950, the Oklahoma state statute providing for segregation of the races in schools had been amended to permit admission of blacks to schools attended by whites in cases where given courses were not available in black schools. A black graduate student thus attended the University of Oklahoma in order to pursue courses leading to a doctorate in education. He was required, however, to sit apart at a designated desk on the mezzanine floor of the library, but not to use the desk in the regular room; and to sit at a designated table and to eat at a different time from the other students in the school cafeteria. Pending an appeal from a lower court decision that found such treatment not to be violative of the Fourteenth Amendment, he was permitted to sit within the classroom in a row specified for colored students; similarly he was allowed to eat in the cafeteria at the same time as other students but he again was assigned to a special table. In ordering all such restrictions removed, the Court held that such separation handicapped the petitioner in his pursuit of graduate instruction:

> Such restriction impairs and inhibits his ability to study, to engage in discussions and to exchange views with other students and in general, to learn his profession, State imposed restrictions which produced such inequality cannot be sustained. . . .
>
> It may be argued that appellant will be in no better position when these restrictions are removed, for he may still be set apart by his fellow students. This we think irrelevant. There is a vast difference—a constitutional difference—between restrictions imposed by the state which prohibit the intellectual co-mingling of students, and the refusal of individuals to co-mingle where the state presents no such bar.[32]

Finally, in *Sweatt v. Painter*,[33] the Court dealt with a situation where the state provided schools for both black and white law students in the State of Texas but petitioner had refused to apply to the black school on grounds that the white university provided substantially better academic opportunities. After a detailed comparison of tangible differences between the schools and such intangibles as reputation of the faculty, experience of the administration, position of influence of the alumni, standing in the community, traditions, and prestige, the Court directed that the petitioner be admitted to the white state school, declaring that "equal protection of the law is not achieved through indiscriminating imposition of inequalities. . . . It is difficult to believe that one who had a free choice between these law schools could consider the questions close." [34]

None of these cases re-examined the separate but equal doctrine as applied to education in terms of segregation's necessary implication of inferiority. But their exploration of the meaning of substantial equality laid a foundation upon which the Supreme Court could reach the conclusion of *Brown v. Board of Education* that separation of the races in state schools was inherently unequal. [35]

Much has been written in support of the position that *Brown* reached the right conclusion for the wrong reasons, [36] or reached the wrong conclusion based on the wrong considerations, [37] or decided the right thing for the right reasons but ordered an ineffective remedy, [38] or ordered the only possible remedy. [39]

Brown does contain language that may be emphasized differently to meet political exigencies. [40] The principal focus, however, was the equal protection clause:

> The most avid proponents of the post-war Amendments undoubtedly intended them to remove all the legal distinctions among "all persons born or naturalized in the United States. . . ." [41]

> Therefore, we hold that the plaintiffs and others similarly situated for whom the actions have been brought are, by reason of the segregation complained of, deprived of the equal protection of the laws guaranteed by the Fourteenth Amendment. [42]

Brown was an effort to eradicate, at least in public education, a pervasive history of discrimination against black Americans. Implementing decisions of the Court have re-emphasized this objective.

In *Brown II*, [43] the Court approved of broad flexible discretion for district courts in devising remedies. District courts were to consider whether the action taken by local school authorities constituted "good faith implementation of the governing constitutional principles." [44] They were to reconcile competing "public and private needs," [45] but the vitality of the constitutional principles was not to be violated or compromised "simply because of disagreement with them." [46] Thus, in *Cooper v. Aaron*, [47] the Court rejected assertions of inability to comply with the decision because of governmental and public resistance:

The constitutional rights of respondents are not to be sacrificed or yielded
to the violence or disorder which have followed upon the actions of the
Governor and the Legislature. . . . "[Promotion of] the public peace by
preventing race conflicts . . . cannot be accomplished by laws or
ordinances which deny rights created or protected by the Federal
Constitution. . . ." In short, the constitutional rights of children not to be
discriminated against in school admission on grounds of race or color
declared by this Court in the *Brown* case can neither be nullified openly
and directly by state legislators or state executive or judicial officers, nor
nullified indirectly by them whether attempted "ingeniously or
ingenuously."[48]

In *Green v. County School Board of New Kent County,*[49] the Court
rejected racially neutral plans for desegregation by offending school officials
that failed to effectively eliminate past practices of segregation. School
officials were obligated to act affirmatively now to comply with the
principles announced in *Brown.*[50]

Further delays in desegregating school systems were rejected in 1969 in
Alexander v. Holmes County Board of Education.[51] And in *Swann v.
Charlotte-Mecklenburg Board of Education*[52] and *Davis v. Board of School
Commissioners of Mobile,*[53] the Court established guidelines for evaluating
plans of desegregation and the means that might be employed to accomplish
this objective.

In *Swann* and *Davis,* the Court again emphasized the equal protection
right of black children in school desegregation cases:

The objective today remains to eliminate from the public schools all
vestiges of state-imposed segregation. Segregation was the evil struck down
by *Brown I* as contrary to the equal protection guarantees of the
Constitution. That was the violation sought to be corrected by the remedial
measures of *Brown II*. That was the basis for the holding in *Green* that
school authorities are "clearly charged with the affirmative duty to take
whatever steps might be necessary to convert to a unitary system in which
racial discrimination would be eliminated root and branch."[54]

School authorities and district courts were directed "to achieve the greatest
possible degree of actual desegregation, taking into account the practicalities of the situation."[55] This could be accomplished by altering attendance
zones, pairing or clustering schools, and transportation of students. The
various remedies, however, were limited if they imposed either risk to the
health of children or significant infringement on the educational process.[56]
The remedies were also limited to the extent of the constitutional violation
established.[57]

Swann and *Davis* marked the merging of constitutional rights and
remedies in school desegregation.[58] Although attempting to establish some
guidelines for school authorities and district courts in future desegregation,

judicial discretion in devising effective decrees for implementation of *Brown* was substantially limited. Thus, in *Bradley v. School Board of Richmond*[59] and *Milliken v. Bradley*,[60] metropolitan desegregation was rejected despite findings that such plans were the only effective means for eliminating state-imposed segregation.[61] Orders directing the merger or crossing of school district lines would be permitted only where it was established that the lines were unconstitutionally drawn or practices of the school districts involved had caused or perpetuated segregation between the districts.

The two *Bradley* decisions and *Swann* and *Davis* inevitably lead to perpetuation of some segregated school districts or individual schools within particular school districts. This had led some to suggest new strategies in school desegregation.[62] Additionally, continued opposition to *Brown* and *Swann* (busing) and conflicting social science studies have led some to suggest that we have reached the limits of school desegregation under equal protection[63] or that more effective alternatives should be explored.[64] We explore then the new strategies or suggested alternatives. We conclude that the only viable means for ensuring equal educational opportunities is through the continued pursuit for desegregation of all schools.

II

Implementation of *Brown* has varied, depending on the persistence of plaintiffs,[65] on the receptivity of the lower court,[66] and, indeed, on public reactions.[67] For more than a decade, courts experimented with pupil assignment acts and freedom-of-choice plans.[68] The initial emphasis was on moving black children to formerly white schools. In addition to the fear of black parents and children to reprisals if they opted to transfer to other schools,[69] there was the expected apprehension that freedom-of-choice plans were designed to place the major burden of desegregation on the victims of discrimination, who were the least able to bear that responsibility.[70] Black schools were being closed;[71] black teachers and principals were being displaced;[72] black children were being discriminatorily suspended and expelled from school;[73] blacks within desegregated schools were subjected to the same racist practices that existed outside the schools.[74] Blacks understandably questioned whether the effort was worth the price.

Additionally, court decisions imposed barriers, as the remedial discretion of district courts was limited. Courts could impose remedies only where constitutional violations were shown. The remedial authority then would extend only to the "limits" of the constitutional violations, although such limitations would not remove all vestiges of state-imposed segregation.[75] Many school districts, therefore, would remain segregated.

Similarly, with the limitations imposed on altering attendance zones, pairing and clustering schools, and busing, and the public opposition to two-way desegregation, some schools within particular districts would remain segregated.[76] Thus in *Northcross v. City of Memphis*,[77] the court approved a plan of desegregation that left more than one-third of the black children in 25 racially identifiable schools. Again, it was understandable for blacks to question the final results after extended efforts at litigation.[78]

It is with these problems in mind that Professor Bell has suggested some alternative strategies.[79] Black parents may consider, he has suggested, using the separate but equal doctrine of *Plessy;* proceedings to ensure representation on school boards; community control of schools; free schools; compensatory education; and tuition funding. He concludes that various alternatives must be pursued in court and politically because "black people cannot expect to find in the *Brown* precedent a full and complete answer to problems that twenty years ago either did not exist in their present form or were not recognizable without the hard-earned contemporary understanding that societal racism can disadvantage black children as effectively (although more subtly) in integrated as in segregated schools."[80]

It is difficult to understand, in view of our past history, how blacks can achieve equal educational opportunities in the segregated schools Professor Bell contemplates. We did not achieve this under *Plessy* and we are not told how equal educational opportunities will be accomplished under present-day societal racism even with new emphasis on separate but equal or representation on or control of local school boards. What *Brown* recognized, as did the decisions leading to *Brown*,[81] was that the history of American racism, including present-day racism, could not be successfully challenged in an apartheid society. Where this practice has the official sanction of the law, and blacks are in no better position to control their destiny than before *Brown*, it is inconceivable that racism will dissipate or abate with blacks in control of or represented on local school boards. There is always the control of that school board and of the schools by a larger school board, the legislature, the courts, and Congress. And if we are pursuing racially separate schools, history has taught us that blacks will inevitably be the losers in the venture, not because of their ability to achieve individually but because they will invariably be denied the basic assets to do so.

Pursuing racially separate and equal educational facilities ignores another finding of *Brown*. The intangibles that flow from desegregated education, both educational and societal, are incapable of duplication in a segregated setting.[82] In one of his numerous opinions in *Swann*,[83] Judge McMillan wrote:

> The essence of the *Brown* decision is that segregation implies inferiority, reduces incentive, reduces morale, *reduces opportunity for association and breadth of experience, and that the segregated education itself is inherently*

unequal. The tests which show the poor performance of segregated children are evidence showing one result of segregation. *Segregation would not become lawful, however, if all children scored equally on the tests.*

I understand that Professor Bell's alternative strategies are based on the assumption that the courts will continue to sanction segregation of some schools and some school districts. The problem, however, is that the strategies perpetuate the myth that equal educational opportunities can be accomplished despite continued separation of the races. In creating or perpetuating this false hope, the suggested strategies invariably inhibit the effort to ensure the objectives of *Brown.*[84]

Because of public opposition and recent social science and educational studies, some writers and some members of the judiciary have suggested that different judicial remedies should be considered. In recent studies, because of growing opposition to busing, James S. Coleman has suggested that the courts have overreached, that the busing orders were adversely affecting education, and that the courts are ill-suited to devise appropriate remedies.[85] In *Keyes v. School Board of Denver,*[86] Mr. Justice Powell suggested that a nationwide, uniform standard for desegregation be decreed. This would respect the interest in neighborhood schools and would reduce busing, although some segregated schools would remain. In addition to imposing a moratorium on busing, Congress has removed from HEW the essential means for ensuring desegregated schools.[87] Other writers have called for studies of alternative means.[88] The vice with all these suggestions is that they contemplate the perpetuation of racially segregated schools—Mr. Justice Powell and Coleman to appease an objecting public, and some writers because they did not find what to them was demonstrative social science research to show that desegregated education was essential to ensure equal educational opportunities.

None of the social science data to date demonstrate that desegregated schools adversely affect black or white students. Those suggesting alternative remedies for desegregation are acting on inconclusive social science data that purport to show that not all the things expected from desegregation have been accomplished. Social scientists, however, do agree that desegregated educational opportunities have resulted in substantial improvement for minority students.[89] Rather than press for alternative remedies under the circumstances, it seems to me that we should be seeking ways of improving educational programs in desegregation settings.

We concede that, under present judicial interpretations, there may remain some districts with racially segregated schools and that in some desegregated systems minority students may for a period continue to experience racist practices. No one to date has suggested a viable alternative to desegregation that would provide an equal educational chance for minority students. Despite the limitations imposed by the judiciary, we have at least in some recent decisions[90] working principles and a variety of remedial tools by which school desegregation may be approached both North and South.

Tremendous progress has been made in the vast majority of southern school districts in dismantling dual school systems. Further efforts to desegregate northern centers are now beginning to bear fruit. Public opposition notwithstanding, we are able today to catalogue many of the various discriminatory practices that have inhibited desegregation. Social scientists and the courts must develop means for countering these reactions to ensure that desegregated educational opportunities are provided for all children. Rather than pursue alternative means for perpetuating a history of discriminatory treatment of minorities, we should concentrate our efforts on future litigation to establish a racially free educational system. If we fail in this objective, we will perpetuate, in the words of Mr. Chief Justice Taney:[91]

> a subordinate class of [blacks] . . . subjected by the dominate race, and, whether emancipated or not, yet subject to their authority . . . [with] no rights or privileges but such as those who hold the power and the government might choose to grant them.

Integration and the self-determination it allows must continue to be the educational goals we pursue.

Notes

[1]347 U.S. 483, 494-495 n. 11 (1954).

[2]See, *e.g.*, *Stell v. Savannah-Chatham County Board of Education*, 220 F. Supp. 667 (S.D. Ga. 1963), injunction granted pending appeal on merits, 318 F. 2d 425 (Fifth Circuit 1963), District Court opinion reversed, 333 F. 2d 55 (Fifth Circuit), cert. den. sub non; *Roberts v. Stell*, 379 U.S. 933 (1964); Wechsler, Toward neutral principles of constitutional law, 73 *Harvard Law Review* 1 (1959).

[3]See, *e.g.*, Armor, The evidence on busing, 28 *Public Interest* 90 (Summer 1972); J.S. Coleman, S.D. Kelly, and J. Moore, "Trends in School Segregation, 1968-73" (Unpublished papers, July 28, 1975, and August 1975, Urban Institute, Washington, D.C.).

[4]*Stell v. Savannah-Chatham County Board of Education, supra*, note 1.

[5]Bell, Waiting on the promise of *Brown*, 39 *Law and Contemporary Problems* 341 (1975); Hawley and Rist, On future implementation of school desegration, 39 *Law and Contemporary Problems* 412 (1975).

[6]For an excellent discussion of judicial implementation efforts, see Read, Judicial evolution of the law of school integration since *Brown v. Board of Education*, 39 *Law and Contemporary Problems* 7 (1975).

[7]Staff of Senate Select Committee on Equal Educational Opportunity, 92d

Cong., 2d Sess., Report, *Toward Equal Educational Opportunity* (Committee Print, 1972).

[8]See R. McKay, "Courts, Congress, and school desegregation," Unpublished paper, U.S. Civil Rights Commission Conference, December 1975.

[9]*E.g., Bradley v. School Board of City of Richmond,* 462 F. 2d 1058 (Fourth Circuit 1972), aff'd by equally divided Court, 412 U.S. 92 (1973); *Milliken v. Bradley,* 418 U.S. 717 (1974); *Carr v. Montgomery County Board of Education,* 377 F. Supp. 1123 (M.D. Ala. 1974), aff'd 511 F. 2d 1374 (Fifth Circuit), rehearing den., 511 F. 2d 1390 (Fifth Circuit 1975), cert. den., 423 U.S. 986 (1975), 46 L. ed. 2d 303 (1975); *Calhoun v. Cook,* 522 F. 2d 717 (Fifth Circuit 1975), rehearing den., 525 F. 2d 1203 (Fifth Circuit 1976).

[10]Bickel, The decade of school desegregation: progress and prospects, 64 *Columbia Law Review* 193, 196 (1964). In commenting on the "deliberate speed" sanctioned in *Brown II,* 394 U.S. 294, 301 (1955), Professor Bickel wrote: "It went without saying . . . that while the vitality of constitutional principles as reflected in specific Court orders ought, to be sure, not be allowed to yield simply because of disagreement with them, disagreement is legitimate and relevant and will, in our system, legitimately and inevitably cause delay in compliance with law laid down by the Supreme Court, and will indeed, if it persists and is widely enough shared, overturn such law."

[11]*Brown I,* 347 U.S. at 492-494.

[12]Pollak, Racial discrmiination and judicial integrity: a reply to Professor Wechsler, 108 *University of Pennsylvania Law Review* 1 (1959); Amaker, *Milliken v. Bradley:* the meaning of the Constitution in school desegregation cases, 2 *Hastings Constitutional Law Quarterly* 349 (1975).

[13]60 U.S. (19 How.) 393 (1856).

[14]*Id.* at 403-404, 416, 426.

[15]Section 1 of the Amendment provides: "All persons born in the United States and subject to the jurisdiction thereof, are citizens of the United States and of the State where they reside. No State shall make or enforce any law which shall abridge the privileges or immunities of citizens of the United States; nor shall any State deprive any person of life, liberty, or property, without due process of law; nor deny to any person within its jurisdiction the equal protection of the laws."

[16]"Neither slavery nor involuntary servitude . . . shall exist within the United States. . . ."

[17]59 Mass. (5 Cush.) 198 (1850).

[18]59 Mass. (5 Cush.) at 209-210.

[19]109 U.S. 3 (1883).

[20]*Id.* at 25.

[21]163 U.S. 537 (1896).

[22]*Id.* at 550.

[23]*Id.* at 551.

[24]*Id.* at 557, 560.

[25]175 U.S. 529 (1899)

[26]*Id.* at 544.

[27]59 Mass. (5 Cush.) 198 (1850).

[28] 163 U.S. 537 (1896).

[29] 305 U.S. 337 (1938).

[30] 332 U.S. 631 (1948).

[31] *McLaurin v. Oklahoma State Regents for Higher Education*, 339 U.S. 637 (1950).

[32] *Id.* at 641.

[33] 339 U.S. 629 (1950).

[34] 339 U.S. at 634-635.

[35] 387 U.S. at 483.

[36] See, *e.g.*, Cahn, Jurisprudence, 30 *New York University Law Review* 150 (1955).

[37] *E.g.*, Wechsler, Toward neutral principles of constitutional law, 73 *Harvard Law Review* 1 (1959); The image of black people in *Brown v. Board of Education*, 1 *Black Law Journal* 234 (1972); Steel, Nine men who think white, *New York Times Magazine*, October 13, 1968.

[38] Carter, Equal educational opportunity, an overview, 1 *Black Law Journal* 197 (1972).

[39] Bickel, *The Least Dangerous Branch: The Supreme Court at the Bar of Politics* 249-254 (1962).

[40] See 347 U.S. at 492-495.

[41] *Id.* at 489.

[42] *Id.* at 495.

[43] 349 U.S. 294 (1955).

[44] *Id.* at 299.

[45] *Id.* at 300.

[46] *Ibid.*

[47] 358 U.S. 1 (1958).

[48] *Id.* at 16. See also *Griffin v. County School Board of Prince Edward County*, 377 U.S. 218 (1964) (local school authorities may not close school districts to avoid desegregation so long as the state maintains free public education for other students in the state); Read, Judicial evolution of the law of school integration since *Brown v. Board of Education*, 39 *Law and Contemporary Problems* 7 (1975).

[49] 391 U.S. 430 (1968). See also *Monroe v. Board of Commissioners*, 391 U.S. 450 (1968); *Raney v. Board of Education*, 391 U.S. 443 (1968).

[50] *Green* represented the first rejection by the Supreme Court of the famous dictum in *Briggs v. Elliott*, 132 F. Supp. 776, 777 (E.D. S.C. 1955) (three-judge court), that *Brown* "does not require integration. It merely forbids discrimination." This dictum had seriously hampered desegregation efforts for more than a decade. Read, *supra*, note 6, at 12-28.

[51] 396 U.S. 19 (1969). See also *Carter v. West Feliciana Parish School Board*, 396 U.S. 290 (1970); Read, *supra*, note 6, at 30-32.

[52] 402 U.S. 1 (1971).

[53] 402 U.S. 33 (1971).

[54] *Swann*, 402 U.S. at 15.

[55] *Davis*, 402 U.S. at 37.

[56] *Swann*, 402 U.S. at 30-31. *Swann*, like *Brown*, contained language that could be

exploited by political exigencies. See *Thompson v. School Board of City of Newport News*, 363 F. Supp. 458 (E.D. Va. 1973), aff'd 498 F. 2d 195 (Fourth Circuit 1974); *Carr v. Montgomery County Board of Education, supra*, note 9; *Calhoun v. Latimer, supra*, note 9.

[57] *Swann*, 402 U.S. at 16.

[58] McKay, *supra*, note 8.

[59] 462 F. 2d 1058 (Fourth Circuit 1972), aff'd by an equally divided Court, 412 U.S. 92 (1973).

[60] 418 U.S. 717 (1974).

[61] See also *Wheeler v. Durham County Board of Education*, 379 F. Supp. 1352 (M.D. N.C. 1974), rev'd on other grounds, 521 F. 2d 1136 (Fourth Circuit 1975). But see *Newburg Area Council, Inc. v. Board of Education of Jefferson County*, 510 F. 2d 1358 (Sixth Circuit 1974), cert. den. 43 U.S.L. Week 3571 (U.S. Sup. Ct. No. 74-1122, April 22, 1975), and *Evans v. Buchanan*, 379 F. Supp. 1218 (D. Del. 1974), *Buchanan v. Evans*, 423 U.S. 963 (1976), cert. den., 46 L. ed. 2d 293 (1976).

[62] *E.g.*, Bell, Waiting on the promise of *Brown*, 39 *Law and Contemporary Problems* 341 (1975). We do not discuss here the *de facto–de jure* distinction. See *Keyes v. School Board of Denver*, 413 U.S. 189 (1973) and Mr. Justice Powell's concurring and dissenting opinion 217-254. For suggestion of abolition of these distinctions, see Fiss, Racial imbalance in the public schools: the constitutional concepts, 78 *Harvard Law Review* 564 (1965); Wright, Public school desegregation: legal remedies for *de facto* segregation, 40 *New York University Law Review* 285 (1965); Silard, Toward nationwide school desegregation: a "compelling state interest" test of racial concentration in public education, 51 *North Carolina Law Review* 675 (1973). We note only in passing that many of the same racial practices and the recognition of the history of pervasive racism noted in *Brown* are equally discernable in the alleged *de facto* segregated school districts. See *Keyes, supra*, at 214-217, concurring opinion of Mr. Justice Douglas; 217-236, concurring and dissenting opinion of Mr. Justice Powell; Fiss, *supra*; Comment, *Keyes v. School District No. 1*: unlocking the Northern schoolhouse doors, 9 *Harvard Civil Rights–Civil Liberties Law Review* 124 (1974).

[63] See, *e.g.*, Read, *supra*, note 6, at 47-49.

[64] *E.g.*, J. S. Coleman, S. D. Kelly, and J. Moore, *supra*, note 3; Hawley and Rist, *supra*, note 5.

[65] Compare *Swann v. Charlotte-Mecklenburg Board of Education*, 402 U.S. 1 (1971), and *Medley v. School Board of City of Danville*, 482 F. 2d 1061 (Fourth Circuit 1973), cert. den., 414 U.S. 1172 (1974), with *Carr v. Montgomery County Board of Education, supra*, note 9 and *Calhoun v. Cook, supra*, note 9.

[66] See *Thompson v. School Board of City of Newport News, supra*, note 55; *Northcross v. Board of Education of Memphis City Schools*, 489 F. 2d 15 (Sixth Circuit 1973), cert. den. 416 U.S. 962 (1974); *Coss v. Board of Education of City of Knoxville*, 482 F. 2d 1044 (Sixth Circuit), cert. den., 414 U.S. 1022 (1973).

[67] See Amaker, *Milliken v. Bradley*: the meaning of the Constitution in school desegregation cases, 2 *Hastings Constitutional Law Quarterly* 349 (1975); Bickel, *supra*, note 10.

[68]Read, *supra*, at 10-20; Knowles, School desegregation, 42 *North Carolina Law Review* 67 (1963).

[69]See U.S. Commission on Civil rights, *Survey of School Desegregation in Southern and Border States, 1965-1966*, pp. 30-44, 51-52 (1966).

[70]*Green, supra*, at 440-442 and n. 5.

[71]*E.g., Allen v. Asheville City Board of Education*, 434 F. 2d 902 (Fourth Circuit 1970). But see *Bell v. West Point Municipal Separate School District*, 446 F. 2d 1362 (Fifth Circuit 1971).

[72]*E.g., Chambers v. Hendersonville City Board of Education*, 364 F. 2d 189 (Fourth Circuit 1966); *Singleton v. Jackson Municipal Separate School District*, 419 F. 2d 1211 (1970).

[73]See, *e.g.*, Children's Defense Fund of the Washington Research Project, Inc., *Children Out of School in America* (1974).

[74]*Jackson V. Marvell School District No. 22*, 425 F. 2d 211 (Eighth Circuit 1970); *Moses v. Washington Parish School Board*, 330 F. Supp. 1340 (E.D. La. 1971), aff'd 456 F. 2d 1285 (Fifth Circuit 1972); *McNeal v. Tate County School District*, 508 F. 2d 1017 (Fifth Circuit 1975).

[75]*E.g., Milliken v. Bradley, supra*, note 9.

[76]*Swann*, 402 U.S. at 22-31. See also *id.* at 31-32: "At some point, these school authorities and others like them should have achieved full compliance with this Court's decision in *Brown I*. The systems would then be 'unitary'. . . . It does not follow that the communities served by such systems will remain demographically stable, for in a growing, mobile society, few will do so. Neither school authorities nor district courts are constitutionally required to make year-by-year adjustments of the racial composition of student bodies once the affirmative duty to desegregate has been accomplished. . . ." *Carr v. Montgomery County Board of Education, supra*, note 9; *Calhoun v. Cook, supra*, note 9.

[77]489 F. 2d 15 (Sixth Circuit 1973), cert. den. 416 U.S. 962 (1974).

[78]The original District Court decision in *Northcross* was rendered on May 2, 1961, the court finding no discrimination, 6 *Race Relations Law Reporter* 428 (W.D. Tenn. 1961), rev'd, 302 F. 2d 818 (Sixth Circuit 1962). Twelve years later, after extensive litigation, the court approved the continued segregation of one-third of the black students.

[79]See Bell, School litigation strategies for the 1970's: new phases in the continuing quest for quality schools, 1970 *Wisconsin Law Review* 257 (1970); Bell, Waiting on the promise of *Brown*, 39 *Law and Contemporary Problems* 341 (1975); Bell, *Race, Racism and American Law* 574-605 (Little, Brown & Co. 1973).

[80]Bell, Waiting on the promise of *Brown*, 39 *Law and Contemporary Problems* 341, 373 (1975).

[81]See discussion *supra*, pp. 32-41.

[82]See also *McLaurin v. Oklahoma State Regents for Higher Education, supra*, note 31; *Sweatt v. Painter, supra*, note 33; Mr. Justice Harlan's dissenting opinion in *Plessy v. Ferguson*, 163 U.S. 537, 557, 560 (1896).

[83]318 F. Supp. 786 (W.D. N.C. 1970), aff'd 402 U.S. 1 (1974) (emphasis added).

[84]See *Calhoun v. Cook, supra*, note 9.

[85]*Supra*, note 3.

[86]418 U.S. 189, 568-589 (1973).

[87]See McKay, *supra*, note 8.

[88]*E.g.*, Hawley and Rist, *supra*, note 5.

[89]See Levin and Moise, School desegregation litigation in the seventies and the use of social science evidence: an annotated guide, 39 *Law and Contemporary Problems* 50 (1975); Weinberg, The relationship between school desegregation and academic achievement: a review of the research, 39 *Law and Contemporary Problems* 240 (1975).

[90]*E.g., Swann v. Charlotte-Mecklenburg Board of Education,* 402 U.S. 1 (1971); *Davis v. School Commissioners of Mobile,* 402 U.S. 33 (1971); *Keyes v. School Board of Denver,* 418 U.S. 189 (1973).

[91]60 U.S. (19 How.) at 405.

Recent Trends in Science Fiction: <u>Serrano</u> Among the People of Number

John E. Coons*

The editors have asked me to comment on the roles played by social science in the school finance cases. I fear that I will not get so far as they had hoped. These are complex questions of epistemology compounded by the abundance of potentially relevant decisions and literature; and thinking about thinking is the hardest thinking I know. But a beginning is possible if examination is limited to a representative few of the recent attacks upon the larger fiscal structures of education, in particular the inter-district challenges such as *Serrano v. Priest*[1] and the *Rodriguez*[2] affair. The focus will be relatively narrow and traditional. Basically, I will ask what social science has done for and can do for the courts in school finance litigation. I begin with a general word about the relation of social science to the values that move judges.

The Sources of Juridical Values

The intellectual operations that mark the judge are distinct from those special to the social scientist (herein often simply "scientist" and his profession "science"). I will define social science broadly as the systematic quest for patterns and regularities in human behavior It is important to emphasize "systematic" in order to distinguish the scientist from the ordinary human observer; the search for patterns and regularities is characteristic not of scientists but of humankind. Further, the distinction

*Time made available by the Childhood and Government Project, Berkeley, was indispensable to the preparation of this paper and is gratefully acknowledged. The author is indebted to Stephen Sugarman and Gail Saliterman for comments on an earlier draft.

between systematic and ordinary inquiry does not lie in the degree of complexity. There is, for example, no process of social discovery more sophisticated than learning one's native language. To apply the epistemology of Tom Lehrer, the task is so simple that only a child can do it. Still, neither the child nor I have qualified as social scientists merely by learning English; there are other kinds of social patterns whose discovery requires methods we do not know and whose precise description often requires another language—mathematics—that we cannot speak.

The scientist (again like the rest of us) looks for patterns that have social relevance. He does not ordinarily count for the sake of counting, but operates from hypotheses that make counting a potentially significant act. What is important to note, however, is that, at least in matters normative, it is not his science that tells him what is relevant. One may speak loosely of the normative power of the actual, but ordinarily this is to be understood only negatively—as the capacity of data to predict impending conflicts among values and thereby to disclose empirical limits to the moral aspirations of society. The aspirations themselves are grounded in non-empirical sources.

For example, empirical observ ition of American society in 1850 would have been impotent either to justify or to condemn the institution of slavery; it might, however, have provided a user il prediction of the costs and benefits of any effort by the Supreme Court to effect its elimination. Social science cannot provide values but, like other bases for prediction, it can suggest the value trade-offs entailed in the court's adoption of this or that decisional norm. This capacity of science to anticipate the consequences of policy change supports the prudential or reflexive element in adjudication; it assists the judge's practical reason. *Rodriguez,* which we will shortly examine, could be read with this role of science in mind.

The ascription of normative relevance to phenomena is, however, a distinctive feature of judicial activity. Legal principles are only one form of the normative—and, in the larger human picture, a secondary one—but they have their importance and in any case happen to be our subject. In the discharge of their special function, courts, unlike scientists, declare principles for human action and restraint. And, unlike the principles that inform our private lives, those uttered by courts authorize the use of force; they link phenomena to government. Courts must, for example, decide whether aliens are entitled to the use of the official power to provide them a public education. The affirmative judicial answer to such a normative question furnishes the occasion for behavioral inquiry concerning the present treatment of complaining aliens.[3]

The non-empirical element in judicial activity is perhaps most obvious when the principle to be selected and applied is constitutional in character.

CARNEGIE LIBRARY
LIVINGSTONE COLLEGE
SALISBURY, N. C. 28144

Insofar as the court passes judgment on the behavior of elected lawmakers, it explicitly subordinates majoritarian values. Judicial review is an institutional limitation upon the normative power of the actual.

The degree to which the court is free to declare new principles depends upon many factors. Obviously, a tightly-drawn cranny in the tax code offers fewer options than the broad poetry of the Fourteenth Amendment. Yet, where the issue before a court is not simply factual, the judge commonly has normative discretion, because the economics of litigation assure that conflicts reaching him are seldom cut and dried. The court, therefore, can—indeed must—create principle in whatever interstices remain.

And "create" is the proper word for this function. Indeed, the utterance of juridical norms resembles in an institutional form the activity of autonomous mind in Kantian epistemology. How close a resemblance I leave to philosophers; I certainly do not mean that judges are independent of their experience any more than they are independent of statute or constitution. They must choose from among the possibilities represented in what they are and know and believe, including patterns and regularities disclosed to them by social science. Without experience—without phenomena delivered to the judicial mind—there is no substance for the work of adjudication. And science is one provider of phenomena. Yet the distinctive act of adjudication is not to perceive behavior but to judge it. The judge acts *from* experience, but the experience and the act of judgment are not linked by necessity. In a deterministic jurisprudence, there may be people called judges, but the label is meaningless.

The judicial history of both school finance and racial discrimination strongly confirms the relative independence of courts from science in the selection of the values to be given expression in the law. In saying this I do not overlook the ambiguous role accorded social science in the original decision to outlaw segregation.[4] I recognize that there is still debate about the significance of that allusion. Nor do I ignore the references in the finance cases to various scientific revelations; I will discuss these shortly. My point for the moment is more basic. I believe that the courts would never have reached the stage of citing Kenneth Clark or Christopher Jencks, unless they had already made a lusty normative leap unaided by anything more than their non-empirical values. These specimens of research were relevant only because judges had already accepted some notion of human equality as a value to be incorporated in the process of judicial rule selection. In some sense wholly undefined, equality had already become a part of the active normative equipment even of the majority in *Rodriguez* who voted against the challengers. The majority's rationale manifestly assumes an equality of human dessert; the system is to be justified as a system worthy of equals. This dynamic of postulated equality goes much further than anything required by the structure of either the Fourteenth Amendment or analogous state formulas (themselves all non-empirical in origin). Indeed, history discloses how narrowly the equal protection guarantee could be construed by a judiciary unconvinced of the moral claims of human equality.

What has science contributed to the ideology of equality as it has penetrated the judiciary? Scientists in their personal roles as social advocates may have exercised great influence, but science as such has been meager on the side of equality. The primary message of the empiricists is that, whatever criterion is employed, people are strikingly diverse in their talents. Even confining our attention to the literature on variations by race, income, or sex, the picture is little different. Of course, much depends on how the relevant talent is defined, on whom you read, and on whom you believe. I am sure that I do not know whether there are significant differences by race, income, or sex. But I am also sure I don't care; or, more accurately, my own commitments to what I mean by equality have nothing to do with empirical findings concerning the distribution of natural talents. And I believe the courts have felt the same. Equality is not an inference from data; it is an act of faith about intrinsic human worth.

Equality will continue to elude the scientists. It need not elude the judges, however, because they remain free, with Jefferson, to hold truths that are "self-evident" and to act upon them. Law remains free, because its informing principle is an ideal; it is science that is indentured to tomorrow's evidence. Now, this is a bondage I admire and would maintain at all cost; someone must remain committed to truth as the ultimate object. But, if I may invoke the shade of Edmond Cahn, I would advise against making our constitutional liberties a function of anybody's science.[5] For the actual sources of those liberties I suggest the ideologies that made our legal tradition. That, however, is not our subject.

Although science cannot disclose to the court its proper object, it may yet be of great importance to the process of adjudication. I would suggest two typical roles for science that were relevant or potentially relevant in the finance cases and may yield some loose generalizations: First, science supplies impact predictions, thereby helping courts to fashion rules for decision that will optimize the values they perceive to be at stake; second, once the decisional rule is selected, science may help prove or disprove alleged violations of that rule. In short, science predicts and science proves. Of course, other kinds of evidence that are not science serve these same functions; science should be distinguished from these not by the manner of its judicial use but by its systematic methodologies.

The Predictive or Prudential Role of Science

The employment of science to predict the consequences of a proposed legal rule is a conventional judicial practice. The court commonly subjects the conflicting rules proffered by the parties to assessment of a prudential sort: Can such a rule be enforced; what portion of finite judicial energies will it require; will it receive public support; what is the economic cost; what other public values must be sacrificed? Not all such considerations appear in the opinions, but in fact, like the rest of us, judges often choose to avoid vain or costly conduct even at the sacrifice of a principle that, other things being equal, would be preferred. Other things are seldom equal, and the court changes the status quo only when it is reasonably confident that settled values—federalism, legislative discretion, enforceability—will not be unduly jeopardized.

Viewed sequentially, the process of rule selection begins with the identification of all the values potentially affected by the proposed rule. The court next invokes whatever sources of prediction are available. It inquires of social science, logic, the sages, and perhaps the muses, what the fate of these values would be under such a rule. Lon Fuller once had one of his make-believe judges include in his written opinion private information gleaned by the judge's niece from the secretary of a public official concerning a probable practical effect of the proposed decision.[6] Fuller implied that this was going a bit far, but I was left wondering whether the judge's sin was more in the relying or in the telling. In any case, I think it is naive to expect that the judicial search for predictive data will be anything but broad where basic values are feared by the judges to be in conflict.

Many of the reflexive or prudential questions encountered by the court in moving toward the selection of a rule for decision are of a sort to which science is relevant; indeed, the examples are potentially infinite. A showing that the elimination of capital punishment is significantly correlated with homicide rates would be prudentially relevant to the settlement of the cruel and unusual punishment question.[7] A demonstration that Chinese children learn English best in the standard curriculum could have been germane in the bilingual education cases.[8]

The inter-district school finance opinions showed varying degrees of interest in one such question—the relation of the cost of an education to its quality. At the threshold there was a definitional question. Quality here could have meant either educational *inputs* measured by dollars and what they buy or *outputs* that can be measured only by discovering how the child has been changed by school. The issue was argued in both forms in several of the cases. In *Rodriguez*, however, the output criterion was given special emphasis by the Supreme Court and has since commanded primary scientific and journalistic attention. The Court in *Rodriguez* worried explicitly about the lack of any scientific demonstration that reform would be worth the trouble. The children may be formally cheated by the system, but, asked the Court, are they significantly worse off in fact? What impact would be wrought by judicial intervention beyond the raising of teachers' salaries?

It is interesting to compare the appellate decisions in *Serrano*, *Robinson*,[9] and *Rodriguez* on this issue. *Serrano* gave it little attention, suggesting its possible relevance in a footnote but giving the trial court no clear direction.[10] Subsequently the trial court took extensive input and output evidence, finding for plaintiffs on both questions but holding that the effect of wealth discrimination upon input was itself sufficient injury to constitute the violation.[11] The California Supreme Court seems likely to affirm this holding. In *Robinson v. Cahill*, the New Jersey Supreme Court affirmed the trial court's findings that money and quality were positively related to both inputs and outputs, but did so in a fashion suggesting that scientific testimony may have been unnecessary; it was enough, perhaps, that the legislature had plainly believed money important to both inputs and outputs. Here is the whole of that court's attention to the issue:[12]

> There was testimony with respect to the correlation between dollar input per pupil and the end product of the educational process. Obviously equality of dollar input will not assure equality in educational results. There are individual and group disadvantages which play a part. Local conditions, too, are telling, for example, insofar as they attract or repel teachers who are free to choose one community rather than another. But it is nonetheless clear that there is a significant connection between the sums expended and the quality of the educational opportunity. And of course the Legislature has acted upon that premise in providing State aid on formulas designed to ameliorate in part the dollar disparities generated by a system of local taxation. Hence we accept the proposition that the quality of educational opportunity does depend in substantial measure upon the number of dollars invested, notwithstanding that the impact upon students may be unequal because of other factors, natural or environmental.

Unlike *Robinson*, however, *Rodriguez* had come to the federal Supreme Court after a trial in which the cost/quality issue had been virtually ignored. Mr. Justice Powell, nonetheless, inquired outside the record for the state of professional opinion. This search proved significant in Powell's eyes, not because he found that science had successfully measured the effect of money, but precisely because there was no settled view. Citing Christopher Jencks and others,[13] he noted:[14]

> On even the most basic questions in this area the scholars and educational experts are divided. Indeed, one of the major sources of controversy concerns the extent to which there is a demonstrable correlation between educational expenditures and the quality of education—an assumed correlation underlying virtually every legal conclusion drawn by the District Court in this case.

Later he added more detailed observations about the state of the art, including the following:[15]

> ... there appear to be few empirical data that support the advantage of any particular pupil-teacher ratio or that document the existence of a dependable correlation between the level of public school teachers' salaries and the quality of their classroom instruction.

This view of its own role and that of science was an interesting departure for the Court. In previous issues of personal rights, it had generally avoided the assessment of consequential injury as a criterion of relief. The right was defined as opportunity, and the denial of the opportunity was in itself the injury. "Output" was not the question. Thus, where a convict sought a free transcript or the appointment of appellate counsel to assist his appeal, the likelihood that these aids would effect a reversal of his conviction was left unconsidered.[16] And, when the Court struck down residential criteria for welfare as a burden on the right to travel, it did so without the slightest empirical evidence of the reality of that burden; indeed, it did so at the request of plaintiffs, who had already traveled to the defendant state in spite of the waiting period.[17]

In this respect *Brown* and *Rodriguez* provide a curious comparison. Each made a casual and untechnical use of science—the one to support, the other to reject, the injury to the school child. One wonders how Edmond Cahn would have reacted to *Rodriguez*. His celebrated comment on the unintended risks of using social science has an uncommonly current ring on the issue of injury to the child:[18]

> There is another potential danger here. It concerns the guarantee of "equal protection of the laws." Heretofore, no government official has contended that he could deny equal protection with impunity unless the complaining parties offered competent proof that they would sustain or had sustained some permanent (psychological or other kind of) damage. The right to equal protection has not been subjected to any such proviso. Under my reading of the *Brown* and *Bolling* opinions, this would remain the law. But if, in future "equal protection" cases, the Court were to hold that it was the expert testimony that determined the outcome of *Brown* and *Bolling*, the scope of the constitutional safeguard might be seriously restricted. Without cataloguing the various possibilities, one can discern at least that some of them would be ominous. It is not too soon to say so, for basic rights need early alarms.

Nothing need be added to Cahn's warning beyond describing what Mr. Justice Powell did in *Rodriguez*. A generation after *Brown* the Court came full circle, now to belittle the interest of the child in acquiring a fuller share of education. As justification for its scepticism about injury, the Court cited the work of social scientists, none of whom had testified and some of whose work (specifically Jencks') was so recent as to prevent cross examination even of the sort provided by professional peers and reviewers in scholarly journals. These works had necessarily been based on the crudest data; and in their conclusions they flatly disagreed with one another as to whether an increase in educational inputs would much improve outputs.

This was a literature that the Court could barely have read, much less mastered. It was literature prepared for a different purpose whose conflicting findings had to be wrenched into relevance. These were given full dignity in the teeth of the factual assumption adopted by the legislature itself and even by the wealthy districts who supported the state's appeal. The Court simply ignored this "common sense" kind of evidence and concluded the matter with a final order, making no provision even for trial of the question, further emphasizing that the discussion is dictum. A more insouciant resolution of such a complex issue is difficult to imagine.

In citing this indeterminate science, does the Court adumbrate some principle concerning proof of consequential injury—and, if so, what principle? What quantum of proof would satisfy such a burden if it were to be cast upon the children? And of what would that proof consist—more treaties on the plaintiffs' side? And proof as to what kind of output—reading scores, income, joy, patriotism?

My guess is that the majority's handling of the cost/quality issue in *Rodriguez* is not likely to become a habit. Consider if you will the same Court's disposition of the parallel problem the following term in *Lau v. Nichols*. Here the issue was perceived to be whether non-English speaking Chinese pupils, by being treated like everyone else in the school system, were suffering discrimination within the meaning of Title VI of the Civil Rights Act of 1964. There is no settled theory about the need for bilingual instruction nor even about its definition; but there is a spirited professional debate. Some experts advocate excusing the child for a period or two a day for special and separate instruction in English. Others would teach him primarily in his first language. There are many other views, including one holding that special arrangements for these pupils do as much harm as good. None of these views had been presented by either plaintiffs or defendants in *Lau*, nor did the Court itself inquire into the state of professional knowledge about the potential or actual injury at stake. This was unnecessary, for, as the Court put it:[19]

> We know that those who do not understand English are certain to find their classroom experiences wholly incomprehensible and in no way meaningful.

That "we know" the effects of thrusting such children into the normal curriculum is more than a little surprising. Before committing itself to such a position, it might have been worth the Court's hearing from learning theorists and educational historians how the immigrant children who populated our public schools in 1920 learned their English. Certainly any justice who had joined the majority in *Rodriguez* would have been expected to inquire concerning the state of scientific knowledge. Perhaps a personal note will be pardoned. At the time *Lau* was decided I had four children who spoke only English enrolled in the local schools of a foreign country, and until I read the Court's opinion, I had thought them blessed for the experience. Of course, theirs was a distinguishable situation, and I do not assert that the Court was wrong in *Lau;* indeed, the Project for which I work filed a brief on the winning side. Maybe the Court was better off for its apparent ignorance of the professional conflict and its intuitive perception of the truth; a little knowledge can be an effective thing.

Is there a principle by which to determine the proper uses of social science in predicting the consequences of judicial rule-making? When should the court "know" the effects of a specific policy, and when should it defer to science? How strong and clear must the scientific answer then be to persuade; and if it conflicts with otherwise relevant and useful non-scientific evidence, is the latter to be disregarded as an inherently inferior form of information? What is the proper view where science itself is deadlocked on a particular question?

I see no answer to these questions other than the application of the ordinary modes of inquiry derived in the long and essentially evolutionary experience of courts in developing rules in the face of varying degrees of indeterminacy as to their impact. There are, of course, several relevant caveats for the judges. One is that, when science is available in the courtroom (or on remand), ordinarily it should be put through its professional paces if it is to be used. The court should assure itself that science has claimed no more than it can demonstrate and that it has sensible standards for what qualifies as a demonstration. And where, as in *Rodriguez*, science has not been before the bench for critical inquiry, the courts should be slow to resort to the library without providing the parties opportunity to challenge the relevance, conclusions, and methodology of the chosen sources. The force of this may be qualified where the matter at issue is either relatively clear or relatively unimportant; no doubt some questions are trivial enough that considerations of judicial economy and other public values should dominate. Perhaps most non-constitutional issues are of this sort (although, thinking of *Lau,* I wonder). But certainly such human rights as freedom from racial discrimination, freedom of speech, and fair criminal process are candidates for protection from the hostile use of unchallenged scientific opinion. For my part the interest at stake in *Rodriquez* was another.

Nor does the fact that an issue is disposed of only in dictum always excuse full diligence by the court. Dictum on a matter such as the burden to show injury could have broad relevance in constitutional law outside *Rodriguez*. Surely there will be other cases in which science will be in similar discord but where the question of injury will be more than dictum. Who then will bear what burden? For example, does the cost/quality conclusion in *Rodriguez* tend to undermine the stability of the result in *Hobson v. Hansen*? To the extent that *Hobson* involves the reshuffling of resources among children of the same race it would seem that plaintiffs might today be required to show that the relatively minor dollar differences there at stake (in comparison to *Rodriguez*) would make a difference in educational outcomes. Still I doubt that any such conclusion was intended and I suggest no principle that would deny the court its use of social science as the basis of dictum so long as that use be well considered.

There is, however, one context for which I can suggest a firmer rule; the cost/quality imbroglio could stand as its prototype. Here there exists a non-scientific basis—indeed a legislative presumption—adequate to determine the issue, whereas science on the contrary finds itself equivocal on the question, either because of conflicting findings or because of the general flabbiness of its methodology. It seems peculiar that the sheer impotence of science should itself disable what is otherwise compelling non-scientific evidence. So to conclude is to value science not for its wisdom but for its very ignorance. That, I fear, was the sin of Justice Powell.

Some Prudential Inquiries for Rodriguez II

The number of possible prudential questions arising out of the inter-district finance cases and potentially involving science is as expansive as the imagination of courts and commentators. And that appears to be considerable. Some critics believe *Serrano* not only to be of no benefit to children's education but actually to threaten social disasters ranging from increases in property tax to the confounding of land use policies to the paralysis of the Court itself. Within the same amicus brief in *Rodriguez* it was warned, first, that spending for public education would fall drastically and, later, that spending would increase dramatically.[20] Justice Powell himself—in this instance without the help of science—hypothesized a conflict between fiscal neutrality and the value of local control; on the basis of this possible threat to a decentralized polity, the state's employment of wealth discrimination was deemed "rational."[21]

Such concern about the probable impacts of judicial intervention—some of it real, or at least intelligible—is today generating serious scientific work that will be available to the state courts in the decade ahead and to the United States Supreme Court when it reconsiders *Rodriguez* in

1986. In addition to its prolonging the unpromising cost/quality debate, science will, I hope, be interested in four kinds of studies that could bear on the courts' ultimate calculus of values and its choice of a decisional norm: (1) Under what circumstances will judicial intervention be necessary to open up the legislative process to consideration of fiscal reform? (2) What judicial techniques can limit the problems of enforcing a judgment of unconstitutionality? (3) What capacity has been shown by reforming legislatures to provide for unusual educational needs? (4) Has legislative fiscal reform so far meant less or more local control?

First, science could help the court by demonstrating through analysis of legislative voting over time whether existing school finance systems represent structural parallels to the apportionment problem. The Court reapportioned the franchise because legislatures were impotent even to address the issue; underrepresented voters had become discrete and insular minorities lacking political recourse. In school finance litigation, plaintiffs' lawyers have asserted (so far without empirics) the following hypothesis: Poor school districts could never generate a legislative majority for reform, because there is nothing for middle-wealth districts in such reform and because the poor districts have nothing to trade for their support. Hence the issue of reform cannot receive a political hearing. The Court is the only authority available to reopen the political system.[22] This hypothesis may be true or false, or true only under some circumstances and in certain states. So far no one has published any serious work on the question. I concede that the methodological problems are substantial.

Second, science should take the opportunity presented by the New Jersey and California cases—and by instances of judicial intervention yet to come—to explore the conditions of effective judicial reform. At one moment, the New Jersey court seems poised to interfere with the distribution of tax collections as a step toward compliance with its mandate in *Robinson*. At the next, it appears to have capitulated to legislative intransigence.[23] It has been argued that the delay and difficulty in New Jersey are a function of the vagueness of the standard adopted to define the violation.[24] If California finally adopts fiscal neutrality this year in the second round of *Serrano*, there may be much to learn in the comparison. The inquiry will not be easy, however, as the political and economic variables are numerous. I will have more to say about the New Jersey problem in the next section.

Third, although it would be technically irrelevant under the decisional norms most likely to be adopted, I believe that the courts will be interested to see whether reforming legislatures have so far shown any sensitivity to the special needs of districts with high costs and to children with special disadvantages. This kind of inquiry will require little more than the monitoring of newly adopted legislated formulas and their intended beneficiaries.[25]

Fourth, the most important scientific inquiries will follow the impact of reform upon local control. Justice Powell took the position that academic nostrums such as power equalizing could not render the state's fears of centralization irrational so long as such reforms remained theoretical models. This posture will become less comfortable if Maine, Wisconsin, and California have working decentralized systems that are fiscally neutral.[26] The analogy to the history of the "exclusionary rule" of criminal evidence is not far-fetched. The experience of those states that had successfully employed the rule could not have been ignored by the Supreme Court when it decided *Mapp v. Ohio.*[27] The same may well be true for the Court's encounters with non-unanimous and undersize juries.

So far the scientific analysis of the impact of power-equalizing systems has been disappointing. Economists seem to assume that even well-intentioned legislatures will adopt formulas that are inappropriate to create fiscal neutrality among their districts. I see nothing in *Serrano,* nor even the practical politics of reform, that impedes the adoption of whatever formula will achieve neutrality in fact. Unless I misread them, the Maine and Wisconsin systems are living examples of neutrality. Thus I react to otherwise useful and able critics like Professor Feldstein with profound frustration.[28] I can imagine that under his or other assumptions a power equalizing formula could favor poorer districts as he predicts. Anything can be badly designed. But why should this be assumed?

The Feldstein empirics have been challenged for inappropriate assumptions and statistical methods.[29] I criticize his work only for its assumption that it is relevant to the wisdom of judicial intervention. If social science is to enter the debates about the likely effects of various reforms—as it should—it ought not to impute to the court anything beyond or different from the principles to which it is explicitly committed. This is not to suggest that, in doing impact predictions, science must confine its inquiry to the issues as the law has cast them. It is at liberty to hypothesize whatever it wishes. But it would be better to make plain that it thereby pursues its own business, not necessarily the law's.

There is a fifth area of impact research that will be very important. This is the issue of the effects of judicial reform on low income families. The manner in which this question arose in *Rodriguez* made it inseparable from the definition of the violation itself, and I would prefer to postpone its discussion to my final section, which deals with the use of social science as proof of violation.

The chances of securing judicial intervention should be enhanced by careful empirical work on these and perhaps other questions involving consequential analysis. Of course this assumes that, when the conclusions appear, either they will support the challenger's legal claim or, if ambiguous, the courts will favor the challengers with the benefit of the necessary presumptions. Neither can be guaranteed and may vary from issue to issue.

Science as Proof of Violation

Here is the setting for the other major role of social science; the court has settled upon the controlling rule—the decisional norm—and now must determine the facts thereby rendered relevant. When the violation of the chosen rule does not appear on the face of the challenged legislation or government practice, science may often assist in its discovery or disproof. The court provides the hypothesis; the scientist provides the evidence: Racial discrimination is forbidden in jury selection; what is the probability that this jury panel was stacked? Children may not be labeled and treated as EMR without adequate reason; does the test used by this school district actually measure the relevant factors? Schools may not systematically provide fewer resources to minority children; how are the resources of this district distributed?

Of course a decisional norm gets us to scientific proof only if it poses scientific questions. And in school finance litigation, this may not always be the case. If the court adopts an input measure of quality, for example, differences in quality may be proved without sophisticated data or statistical inferences. And in many cases there may be no factual question posed at all. Indeed, some of the most important challenges already litigated were structured simply as formal normative conflicts. By this I mean that the rule proposed is in explicit conflict with the challenged legislation or governmental practice. Suppose, for example, a court were to adopt a principle of equal spending as the constitutional rule. In most states the structure of the finance legislation would conflict on its face with this rule, for it guarantees not equal but unequal spending. Since the judicial norm is a constitutional one, the legislation is void. Explicit racial segregation is an historic example of such formal conflict; once the new governing constitutional rule had been declared by the Warren Court, the inference of illegitimacy required no empirical mediation. The social science in *Brown* went only to the question of the rule to be adopted; once adopted, no scientific question remained.

The *Serrano* norm of fiscal neutrality appears to have this same quality in relation to the present legislated structures. The state code provisions for taxing, spending, and partial equalization assume on their face that there is to be an influence of school district wealth upon spending. Hence, the normative conflict is formal, and proof is reduced to the official arithmetic of assessed valuations, taxing, and spending. Indeed, in theory even these figures may be unnecessary except to dramatize the injustice and spark the court's enthusiasm for imposing the quietus.

Given a rather unusual set of empirical assumptions, however, this prima facie appearance of formal conflict could be false. It is possible to imagine a set of conditions in which the present model of local government would be fiscally neutral. Indeed, this has been imagined in the economic literature if not in the litigation. As Reischauer and Hartman have suggested,[30] a wholehearted adoption of the "Tiebout hypothesis" might be thought to satisfy *Serrano*. Professor Tiebout[31] would have us view the menagerie of decentralized local governments as a market in public services that consumers purchase along with their residence. If residential prices and rents accurately reflect the property tax burden and the quality of public services that tax supports, there is a rough approximation of the fiscal neutrality that would be achieved under a district power-equalized system. It is not my present purpose to evaluate the merits of this hypothesis. My point is that in theory the conflict of the legislation with the constitutional norm could be prima facie only and, therefore, that science should be permitted, if it can, to overcome the plain import of the statute.

Indeed, even a constitutional principle of equal spending could be shown to be unoffended in practice; take, for example, the possible (although grossly improbable) case that offsetting differences in district wealth and tax rates would in some states produce essentially uniform spending. Spending disuniformity is, of course, simple to prove and ordinarily conceded by the state. It is certainly not a matter requiring social science. The Tiebout hypothesis, on the other hand, would require sophisticated economic data for its demonstration. This could explain its otherwise curious absence from *Serrano* and *Rodriguez*. (My guess is that it was overlooked by defendants.) That the hypothesis is merely unprovable and intuitively wrong would not be enough to exclude it, as we learned from Justice Powell's handling of other empirical assertions that seem to conflict with both good sense and legislative assumptions. I feel tactically safe in raising Tiebout, because my distinguished colleagues, Charles Benson and Gareth Hoachlander, expect to have something empirical—and I hope nasty—to say about the Tiebout proposition in a year or so. In any event, the hypothesis exemplifies a potential employment of social science—to eliminate a formal normative conflict by demonstrating that in fact the system already does just what the constitutional challengers would require of it.

Assuming now that Tiebout is wrong, substantially wrong, or unprovable, neither a fiscal neutrality nor an equal spending rule would need the support of scientific proof to establish violation. However, several quite different proposed constitutional formulas have appeared in one context or another in the school finance area that for proof of violation might require science of varying content and sophistication. Three of these proposed rules actually made their appearance in various ways in judicial opinions, one achieving recognition as state law. Each represents a misperception of the character and limits of judicial review of legislation. Where the object is major structural change, the rule should be one amenable to simple proof. A rule requiring vaguely defined or sophisticated empirical proof is unlikely to be adopted; if adopted, it is unlikely to be enforced against a reluctant legislature. Let us review the examples.

The problem appeared early in the history of the finance litigation. The very first attacks on state fiscal structures in 1968-1969 proposed the rule that each child's individual need for educational resources is the measure of his federal constitutional entitlement.[32] Had the federal courts entertained this view, a fair portion of the social science professions could have become engaged in litigation on a full time basis advising courts how to define need and declaring what each child needed and how much of this he was not getting. Fortunately, in my judgment, the proposal received short judicial shrift.

The second constitutional rule requiring complex and largely undefined scientific proof appeared in *Robinson v. Cahill*.[33] There the court adopted as the basis of a personal right a previously undisturbed metaphor in the New Jersey Constitution. The child of that state now holds constitutional entitlement to a "thorough and efficient" education. In its original opinion and in four separate subsequent decisions filling hundreds of pages with majority opinions, dissents, and innumerable essays, the court has made little progress in specifying the fault in the system beyond this inscrutable phrase.

Robinson illustrates that losing lawsuits is not the only risk created by employment of such vague formulas. Where the court cannot clearly specify the wrong—where its invalidation of the existing order remains essentially unprincipled—it may expect an unprincipled response from both social science and the legislature. That appears to have been the essential reaction to *Robinson*. The opinions and the literature on the case disclose a kaleidoscope of unrelated empirics and conflicting policy proposals presented by social science to the court and to a puzzled legislature, each proposal as plausible as any other in its claim to be "thorough and efficient." The reaction of the New Jersey legislature has been wholly consistent; given an unscrutable mandate, it has responded in kind.

The denouement, however, seems at hand. In 1976, the New Jersey Supreme Court, in its fifth set of opinions, has approved as "thorough and efficient" a newly enacted school finance system, one that is the match of its predecessor in giving preference to rich districts. The court appears to have capitulated. I say "appears" only because the meaning of this *per curiam* opinion, like that of its four predecessors, simply eludes the grasp. It is, nonetheless, sufficiently plain that no substantial change has been or will be effected by this interminable litigation despite an avalanche of scientific assistance. The problem has been, perhaps, that science gave the court precisely what it asked for—information unmediated by any central intelligible proposition. The decision was a political act in the political mode; the court and the children were bound to lose.

A third example of a decisional rule forcing improvident employment of social science appears in *Rodriguez* itself. The manner in which *Rodriguez* was tried and argued, including the nature of the empirical data presented by plaintiffs, made it possible for the federal Supreme Court to treat the case as if there were a serious factual allegation left wanting scientific proof. The problem had to do with the definition of wealth. The plaintiffs had never been able to settle clearly upon the role of poverty in their theory. From before the filing of the earliest complaint in Detroit in February 1968 even until today there has been strong disagreement among counsel in all the finance cases as to whether and how personal income should play a part in the definition of the injured class. Those who provided the argument for *Serrano* took the following view: Personal poverty probably does increase the injury to the individual living in a poor district because of the inability of the lower income family to purchase private substitutes; but the constitutional wrong should not be defined in terms of personal wealth but as the relative poverty of the tax bases of state-created school districts. Irrespective of how low income families may prove to be distributed within the various states, there are plenty living in low wealth school districts; it would be an eccentric and unprincipled policy that would hope to assist poor children by maintaining the privilege of rich school districts in which by chance some of them live. Equally important, the Court is unlikely to adopt a rule employing the subtle definitions and complex scientific proof required by concepts of personal wealth.

The constitutional issue had been resolved earlier on this simpler basis in *Serrano,* which had held that disparities in district wealth were enough to show the violation.[34] Nevertheless, in *Rodriguez* plaintiffs chose to confuse, or at least to complicate, the issue by introducing as evidence of constitutional violation a supposed correlation between district poverty and personal poverty.[35] The evidence seemed of dubious relevance and not very persuasive to the Supreme Court. It was rendered even less so by the appearance of a study of the relation of personal to district poverty in Connecticut by the editors of the *Yale Law Journal.*[36] The majority opinion in *Rodriguez* described this study as "exhaustive" and quoted its conclusion that in Connecticut "the major factual assumption of *Serrano*—that the educational financing system discriminates against the 'poor'—is simply false."[37]

The Court did not misread *Serrano* so badly as did the *Yale* editors. Mr. Justice Powell showed in one paragraph that he in fact understood (and rejected) the clear and simple poverty definition embodied in fiscal neutrality. In any case, the result in *Rodriguez* probably would not have differed if the question of where the poor live had never been raised. The decision was based a good deal more on the majority's values than on the state of science. Yet one can wonder. The *Yale* "findings" made it possible for the majority to emerge from *Rodriguez* looking almost as if it had protected from fatuous intermeddling a special privilege enjoyed by poor families under the existing system. Perhaps someone among the majority even believed this and gave it weight. During oral argument, one concurring justice recalled that, when he was a boy, the fanciest schools in his state were in the mining towns where the ethnic minorities were clustered.[38] Presumably he saw the issue as personal poverty; perhaps he continued to do so until the end.

After *Rodriguez* was decided, it was discovered by Grubb and Michelson that the *Yale* comment was seriously in error as to both methodology and empirical conclusions.[39] Not only is there a substantial overall correlation of personal and district wealth in Connecticut, but the Yale editors had been wrong even on the location of the welfare poor. Dean Clune has demonstrated the same relationships for Illinois.[40] Inquiries in 1969 suggested a slightly different pattern in California, but much depends on the definitions employed,[41] and the national pattern, if any, remains to be charted.

The problem of the constitutional role, if any, of personal poverty is a difficult one. Clune and others have shown its several empirical faces; here I will go no further than briefly to suggest what I conceive to be the wisest employment of the data. I continue to believe that the constitutional standard the courts will and should ultimately accept is fiscal neutrality based on whatever is the official measure of local taxable wealth; ordinarily this is taxable property per pupil. That definition of wealth should be left uncomplicated and unrefined by any incorporation of family income in the description of the alleged violation except where the local source of revenue becomes a tax on income. It is unlikely that poverty can be defined to the satisfaction of the court once we pass beyond the simple arithmetic of the official system.

Some assert that only by defining the class in terms of personal poverty can a doctrinal link be forged with judicial precedent. Perhaps this is so, but, if it were thought necessary as a doctrinal matter to employ personal wealth in the legal standard, I would prefer to argue as follows: Wealth is the capacity to purchase a specific good; here that good is education. Wealth, however, must be defined differently for purposes of private and public education. One buys private education with private wealth; he is education-poor in the private market when his personal income is inadequate to afford tuition. One buys public education only with public money; he is education-poor in the public market if his school district is poor. In the case of public education, personal wealth and district wealth are *identical*, because the only wealth a family has available for the purchase of public education is that of its school district. If my district is poor, I am poor insofar as my ability to purchase public education is concerned. Analytically it is hard to know what else could be meant by "personal" poverty in relation to the purchase of public education. So far as proof of the constitutional violation is concerned, it is proper literally to identify district poverty with personal poverty.

This approach would eliminate science from the litigation insofar as proving the violation is concerned; proof would be at most a matter of the official arithmetic of assessed valuation. The basic constitutional standard would remain clear and manageable. Yet, Clune and others are perfectly correct in thinking that the courts will be interested in the actual impact of the adoption of fiscal neutrality on lower income persons, families, and children—that vague class for which judges have historically shown a measure of special concern. But, as I have argued, violation of the decisional norm is one question, and the impact of judicial intervention is quite another. Regarding poverty, the proof of the constitutional wrong should be sharply distinguished from predictions of the consequences. The manifest and crucial role of social science here is not to show the violation of the decisional norm but to prepare a map of lower-income families for each of the fifty states that will permit the intelligent appraisal by the Court of the probable consequences of judicial intervention for various income classes. And in defining such classes, science should exercise all the freedom it needs. There is a good deal more leeway and ambiguity to be tolerated in the selection of what is relevant when science is predicting consequences than when it is determining the violation of a standard fixed by the court for deciding the dispute.

Ambiguous decisional standards promise to remain a problem. An example is the current "urban Serrano" in New York.[42] The parties there are preparing for trial in a suit attacking discrimination against New York City pupils, a discrimination alleged to be the consequence of the state system of school finance. New York City has a high assessed value per pupil and spends about $2400 per year. Plaintiffs, however, hope through social science to demonstrate that, when municipal overburden, high costs, special pupil needs, and other factors are accounted for, the city's children somehow are being cheated. If the court is willing to receive a mountain of scientific data, definitions, and expert opinions from both sides, the trial may become—like *Robinson v. Cahill*—an interesting seminar in school finance and local government. That it will result in a judgment for plaintiffs seems doubtful given the near total absence of legal standards by which to judge the system. And I do not perceive how any quantum of science can make up for the normative vacuum.

The point in all this is not that science is inherently unsuited to provide evidence of violations in school finance cases. Obviously everything depends on the nature of the particular dispute and the decisional norm appropriate to its resolution. Many situations have already arisen or could be imagined in which science was or would be crucial to proof of the violation. In some of the school exclusion cases (if these be "school finance" issues), science played an indispensable role in exposing the misuse of administrative criteria that were either improperly excluding children from school, misassigning them to schools or classes for the retarded, or relegating them to lower tracks on the basis of culturally biased and wholly inadequate test instruments.[43] In these cases, the scientist was given a reasonably clear question about the efficacy of testing and/or its application to individual children.

Likewise, in intra-district finance litigation such as *Hobson II*,[44] Judge Wright was able to put to the parties a set of empirical questions at a level neither too simple nor too abstruse. Economists could respond in a professional manner, and their answers would help determine the questions of violation. In the end, the clash between experts generated conceptual conflicts that went beyond the "moral and constitutional arithmetic" finally adopted by the court; yet it appears that the contribution of the experts to understanding the relevant empirical situation was substantial.

Ultimately, questions of constitutional violation requiring scientific proofs may reappear even in inter-district litigation. No one can predict how various states will define the legal questions under their own constitutions; certainly fiscal neutrality will not be the only principle promoted by reformers. Even if it were, in some future test of a reformed system it might become relevant to incorporate in the definition of wealth such elements of "wealth" as geographical cost differences. That issue alone could give useful and interesting employment to many an economist.

Conclusions

There is a rich mine of scholarly and analytical opportunities in this area, only a few of which have been noted here. My own approach has been to ask what science should and should not be asked to do for courts; but this is the relatively narrow perspective of a lawyer, and one who has a policy axe to grind. There are a dozen other approaches, some more academic, others holding promise of fairly immediate policy relevance.

One could approach the judicial behavior involved in these recent cases as itself a matter fit for scientific analysis within a paradigm supplied by game theory or small group politics. Or the material could be organized according to professional disciplines—economics, learning theory, political science, and sociology. It could, on the other hand, be approached through each of its substantive contents—the cost-quality issue, the coincidence of personal and district poverty, the modeling of power equalized systems. Still another question is the insight to be gleaned from comparative case studies, illustrating the strategies and gropings of social scientists and lawyers in particular litigation. It would be particularly useful to compare in detail the legal-scientific strategy in the New Jersey and California cases, which differed so greatly; indeed, I believe such a study is contemplated.

Most of all, I hope that all of you will venture beyond the fascinating technical issues and attempt for yourselves a systematic response to the warning of Edmond Cahn. It is wisdom to ask and to continue to ask at what point the court's deference to science becomes the surrender of an important outpost of judicial responsibility. At least where science is locked in basic conflict, there must be a more principled judicial approach than the refusal to consider the issue even on non-scientific grounds. *Silent leges inter armas* is no maxim for the civil wars of social science.

Notes

[1]*Serrano v. Priest*, 5 Cal. 3d 584, 487 P. 2d 1241 (1971).

[2]*San Antonio Independent School District v. Rodriguez*, 411 U.S. 1 (1973). I will also touch on the *Hobson* intra-district variety [*Hobson v. Hansen*, 269 F. Supp. 401 (D.D.C. 1967), aff'd in part and appeal dismissed in part, sub nom *Smuck v. Hobson*, 408 F. 2d 175 (D.C. Cir. 1969); and see *Hobson v. Hansen*, 327 F. Supp. 844 (D.D.C. 1971)] and refer briefly to problems of exclusion from school—actual and virtual—in particular *Lau v. Nichols*, 414 U.S. 563 (1974), the bilingual education case.

[3]*Hosier v. Evans*, 314 F. Supp. 316 (D.V.I. 1970).

[4]*Brown v. Board of Education*, 347 U.S. 483, at 494 (1954).

[5]E. Cahn, Jurisprudence (Annual survey of American law), 30 *New York University Law Review* 150, 157-168 (1955).

[6]L. Fuller, The case of the speluncian explorers, in *The Problems of Jurisprudence* 24 (Temporary ed.; Cambridge: Foundation Press, 1949).

[7]See *Furman v. Georgia*, 408 U.S. 238 (1972). Note the contrasting uses of social science, "experience," and "common sense" in the concurring opinions of Mr. Justice Marshall, 408 U.S. at 348-353, 373-374, and Mr. Justice White, 408 U.S. at 311-314. See also Professor Posner's discussion of the risks of the uses of social

science in these cases in *The Economic Approach to Law* (Coral Gables: Law and Economic Center, 1976).

[8]*Lau v. Nichols, supra,* note 2. See also *Serna v. Portales Municipal Schools,* 351 F. Supp. 1279 (D.N.M. 1972).

[9]*Robinson v. Cahill,* 62 N.J. 473, 303 A. 2d 273 (1973). See also *Robinson v. Cahill,* 63 N.J. 196, 306 A. 2d 65 (1973); *Robinson v. Cahill,* 67 N.J. 35, 335 A. 2d 6 (1975); *Robinson v. Cahill,* 67 N.J. 333, 339 A. 2d 193 (1975); *Robinson v. Cahill,* 69 N.J. 449, 335 A. 2d 129 (1976).

[10]5 Cal. 3d at 601, 487 P. 2d at 1253 (f.n. 16).

[11]*Serrano v. Priest,* unpublished opinion (Los Angeles Sup. Ct., decided Aug. 30, 1974).

[12]62 N.J. at 481, 303 A. 2d at 277.

[13]C. Jencks, *Inequality* (New York: Basic Books, 1972). And see others cited, 411 U.S. at 43 (f.n. 86).

[14]411 U.S. at 43 (f.n. 86).

[15]411 U.S. at 47 (f.n. 101).

[16]*Griffin v. Illinois,* 351 U.S. 12 (1956) transcript); *Douglas v. California,* 372 U.S. 353 (1963) (counsel on appeal). In *Douglas,* the right to counsel was recognized even though the state had established a procedure for distinguishing between cases where counsel would and would not be helpful to appellant.

[17]*Shapiro v. Thompson,* 394 U.S. 618 (1969).

[18]E. Cahn, *Supra,* note 5, at 168.

[19]414 U.S. at 566.

[20]Brief of Liebman, *et al.,* at 54 and 99.

[21]411 U.S. at 49-55. Powell added a general warning that the Court's intervention would generate "an unprecedented upheaval in public education. . . . There is nothing simple or certain about predicting the consequences of massive change. . . ." 411 U.S. at 56.

[22]Clune, Wealth discrimination in school finance, 68 *Northwestern University Law Review* 651, 671 (1973).

[23]See discussion of the court's most recent decision below at pp. 64-65.

[24]J. Coons, Fiscal neutrality after *Rodriguez,* 38 *Law and Contemporary Problems* 299, 306-307 (1974).

[25]See, *e.g.,* the forthcoming chapter by Robert Bothwell, Geographic adjustments to school aid formulae, in Callahan and Wilken (eds.), *School Finance Reform: A Legislators' Handbook* (National Conference of State Legislatures, 1976). Bothwell carefully and convincingly demonstrates that fears that reforming legislatures would overlook the special problems of urban areas have so far proved unfounded.

[26]See W. N. Grubb, The first round of legislative reforms in the post-*Serrano* world, 38 *Law and Contemporary Problems* 459 (1974).

[27]367 U.S. 643 (1961).

[28]M. Feldstein, Wealth neutrality and local choice in public education, 65 *American Economic Review* 75-89 (1975).

[29]W. N. Grubb, The effects of district power equalizing: comments on "Wealth neutrality and local choice in public education," occasional paper, The Childhood and Government Project, Berkeley (1975).

[30]Robert D. Reischauer and Robert W. Hartman, *Reforming School Finance* (Washington, D.C.: Brookings Institution, 1973).

[31]C. M. Tiebout, A pure theory of local expenditure, 64 *Journal of Political Economy* 416 (1956).

[32]*McInnis et al. v. Shapiro et al.*, 293 F. Supp. 327 (N.D. Ill. 1968) aff'd sub nom. *McGinnis v. Ogilvie*, 394 U.S. 322 (1969).

[33]*Supra*, note 8.

[34]5 Cal. 3d at 601; 487 P. 2d at 1252-1253.

[35]411 U.S. at 15.

[36]Note, A statistical analysis of the school finance decisions: on winning battles and losing wars, 81 *Yale Law Journal* 1303 (1972).

[37]411 U.S. at 23, quoting 81 *Yale Law Journal* at 1328-1329.

[38]Mr. Justice Blackmun, Transcript of argument, p. 21.

[39]W. N. Grubb and S. Michelson, Public school finance in a post-*Serrano* world, 8 *Harvard Civil Rights-Civil Liberties Law Review* 550 (1973).

[40]W. H. Clune, Wealth discrimination in school finance, 68 *Northwestern University Law Review* 651 (1973). Clune describes a statistical model for the relation of family income and district wealth that appears replicable for any state.

[41]Coons, Clune, and Sugarman, *Private Wealth and Public Education* 357 (1970).

[42]*Board of Education, Levittown Union Free School District, Nassau County, et al. v. Ewald B. Nyquist, Commissioner of Education et al.* (Filed in the Supreme Court, State of New York, County of Nassau, 1974).

[43]*Hobson v. Hansen, supra,* note 2; *P.A.R.C. v. Commonwealth,* 334 F. Supp. 1257 (E.D. Pa. 1971), 343 F. Supp. 279 (E.D. Pa. 1972); *Mills v. Board of Education,* 348 F. Supp. 866 (D.D.C. 1972); *McMillan v. Board of Education,* 430 F. 2d 1145 (Second Circuit 1970); *Larry P. v. Riles,* 348 F. Supp. 1306 (N.D. Cal 1972); *Lau v. Nichols, supra,* note 2.

[44]327 F. Supp. 844 (D.D.C. 1971).

Social Science and Social Policy: Schools and Race

David K. Cohen
Janet A. Weiss*

Introduction

The last twenty years were halcyon ones for research on education and race. National racial policy advanced after *Brown,* and as efforts to eliminate segregation and discrimination multiplied, research on the problems prospered. What was a trickle of studies in the few years before 1954 became something of an academic torrent.[1] Some of this work has been disinterested but most of it has been, in the inelegant contemporary jargon, policy-oriented.

Research and policy have thus gone hand in hand: as efforts to eliminate segregation moved closer to center stage, research on the problem multiplied. In part this was the result of government efforts to promote studies of current policy, and in part it was due to the fact that researchers' priorities are influenced by what they read in the papers. This entanglement between research and policy was as much a reflection of changing intellectual and social currents as it was the consequence of deliberate efforts to guide the study of social problems.

In any event, the contacts between race research and policy increased. Researchers regularly found themselves testifying in courtrooms, evaluating government programs, or consulting with educational agencies.[2] Sometimes they even found themselves in the newspapers, and more often in the various magazines that publish popular science. Through all this, research on

*The research for this paper was supported partly by grants from the Carnegie Corporation of New York to the Center for Educational Policy Research, Harvard University, and by the American Jewish Committee to the Huron Institute.

education and race improved. Not only did it increase, but in general it grew better, in all the usual ways researchers recognize. Methodology is now more sophisticated than it was twenty years ago. Basic concepts have been overhauled and refined, and new distinctions hatched. Various central scientific hypotheses have been weighed—some, perhaps, have even been tested. Evidence has accumulated at a startling pace, and some of it has been analyzed. Certainly a much broader variety of analytic skills have been devised and used. And finally, efforts to connect research and policy have multiplied, motivated by government, by private foundations, and by many researchers' desires for relevance.

But although research has improved and its contacts with policy multiplied, it has only produced new arguments and complications. As a result, it has not become more helpful for particular policy decisions. Research has proliferated, but so have arguments among researchers: see, for example, the recent spats between Pettigrew and Armor,[3] or between Coleman and Farley.[4] Methods of study have improved, but the results are less accessible: how many of the people who could read the Social Science Brief filed in *Brown*, for example, could also read the Coleman Report's sections on integration and school effects?[5] Research projects have multiplied, but so have competing ways of defining problems and interpreting results: who can decide whether Jencks, Smith, Armor, Coleman, or Pettigrew[6] is right about school integration's effects? In our view, this is not the fault of bad research, nor do we think this situation could be remedied by better research: the prosperity of research quite naturally contributes to a sense of growing complexity, and to confusions over policy advice.

That, indeed, is the theme of this essay: for the most part, the improvement of research on social policy does not lead to greater clarity about what to think or what to do. Instead, it usually tends to produce a greater sense of complexity. This result is endemic to the research process. For what researchers understand by improvement in their craft leads not to greater consensus about research problems, methods, and interpretation of results, but to more variety in the ways problems are seen, more divergence in the ways studies are carried out, and more controversy in the ways results are interpreted. It leads also to a more complicated view of problems and solutions, for the progress of research tends to reveal the inadequacy of accepted ideas about solving problems.

The ensuing complexity and confusion are naturally a terrific frustration, both to researchers who think they should matter and to officials who think they need help. Researchers are thus often taken to task by public officials.[7] More often still, they do it to each other.[8] The ensuing lectures have a monotonous similarity. They urge more refined methods, more attention to the problems of policy-makers and less to those of professors, and more clarity in interpretation. Although we would not interfere with these diversions, we think the frustration and ensuing crossfire of lectures probably results from a misapprehension about the research process. The expectation of direct policy guidance from social research assumes that knowledge in the social sciences is convergent. It is expected that as knowledge improves, there will be more scientific agreement about the issues in question. But knowledge in the social sciences generally is not convergent. Rather than picturing the research process as scouts converging on a target, it might make more sense to picture it as outriders offering different visions of what passes them by. Multiplying the outriders tends to multiply the visions—up to a point, of course. And sharpening their sight tends to refine their differences.

Thus, if the result of scientific improvement in some aspects of physical science is convergence—at least for a time, within important conceptual limits[9]—the result of improvement in the social sciences is a richer, more diverse picture of things. Naturally enough, if one expects the first and gets the second, one is bound to be disappointed, even angry. But it may make sense to locate the trouble in the expectation of convergence rather than in the science. One point of this essay is to propose this view of social policy research and to suggest the criteria of research quality we think it implies. Another is to explain why problems occur when policy-making agencies like courts try to use social research in making decisions.

But we will do both largely by implication. Our chief aim is to illustrate how the research process works in the case of schools and race, and to offer a few ideas about why things turn out as they do. The essay will be organized around these ideas; we have three main points in mind. The first is that, as research on social policy matures, the terms of the problem tend to shift. This owes something to the critical and questioning nature of research, for it often reveals inadequacies in accepted views of a social problem. It also owes something to practical experience, for efforts to solve social problems inevitably turn up unexpected and puzzling results. These are puzzles that research excellently reports, amplifies, and embellishes. In either event, the development of research on any major social problem is a story of continuing redefinition. This rather impedes convergence in scientific opinion.

A second point is that the improvement of research methods tends to increase divergence in the treatment of evidence, and to multiply mystification in the interpretation of findings. Methodological sophistication is a cardinal academic virtue, and is widely regarded as a key to the improvement of policy-relevant research. But such improvements do not increase consensus on research issues. Rather, they clarify differences, reveal previously unsuspected problems in data and analysis, and progressively remove research from the everyday world in which most judges, legislators, and bureaucrats walk and think. Beautifying our avenues of inquiry thus makes the path more Byzantine, the directions more arcane, and the family arguments over the map sharper. Methodological advance creates new dimensions of research virtuosity and argumentation, and this hardly facilitates convergence in scientific opinion.

A final point is that, as research on a social problem matures, the angles of vision multiply. Social problems typically are framed initially in terms of a particular discipline, profession, or research tradition. But as research on a problem prospers, other traditions and disciplines are drawn in. Each involves a different angle on social reality, or different assumptions about how social investigations should be carried out. The result is a richer and more diverse vision of the problem and its possible remedies. But again, this is hardly the stuff of which scientific agreement is made.

Shifting Social Problems

In the beginning, the problem was lawful school segregation. The years immediately surrounding the *Brown* decision saw little ambiguity on this point, even though there was enormous controversy over the issue. According to the research centering on that decision, the legally mandated system of racially dual schools was a problem because it damaged the persons and impaired the opportunities of black Americans. There was little mention of segregation's effects on white persons. And the discussion of remedy was cast in similar terms: eliminating the socially stigmatized black institutions and mixing blacks into the population of white schools.[10]

There was not a great deal of evidence underlying these points: the research was often thin, and the ratio of speculation to empirical findings was sometimes remarkably high. But for all this there was not much diversity of opinion. The main division lay between those researchers who thought segregation was the problem and those who thought it was the solution. In the years just preceding and following *Brown*, resistance to desegregation was the big news; race researchers felt they had a taste of this medicine in the work of social scientists who espoused the genetic inferiority of Negro Americans, and the impossibility of successful desegregation. Henry Garrett and Audrey Shuey[11] were the principal offenders on this point, and they seemed to many only the scientific manifestation of the virulent racism that promoted massive resistance and interposition in Southern politics. Most of the arguments in early desegregation lay between these exponents of racial inferiority and everyone else.

In 1976 there is no such consensus. The doctrine of inherited inferiority among blacks continues to find adherents in the academy, and most researchers continue to oppose such ideas. But they cannot agree on much else. One reason for this was that, in the intervening twenty years, a good deal of desegregation had occurred. This brought southern schools closer to compliance with the Constitution, but it did not produce the other results that earlier law and social science had suggested. In particular, desegregation did not have the expected effects on school performance. The news on this point accumulated slowly throughout the early 1960's, as a modest number of districts desegregated. By the middle of the decade, there were a few reports, which presented very mixed results. In some cases desegregation seemed to be associated with gains in achievement and in some cases it was not. But in no cases were the gains substantial, certainly not enough to have much effect on black-white achievement differences.[12]

In the summer of 1966, *Equality of Educational Opportunity*[13] (the so-called Coleman Report) was dropped, rather like a long-acting repeating bomb, into this moderately confused scene. The survey reported that racial segregation had no independent impact on Negro school achievement. Schools' social class composition did seem to affect achievement, and since Negro Americans were disproportionately poor, liberals reasoned that social class integration would result in racial integration.[14] How this might be related to earlier research or legal ideas about racial segregation, though, was never terribly clear. And finally, the Coleman Report found no consistent relationship between school desegregation and racial attitudes. The net effect, then, was to call into question several accepted ideas about race and schools.

The next major study did not help. The U.S. Civil Rights Commission undertook a Presidentially-commissioned analysis of northern school segregation,[15] and the results were a little curious. The Commission accepted Coleman's findings about the non-effects of schools' racial composition, but found, in further analysis of the Coleman Report data, that racially integrated classrooms had a positive effect on achievement—in high school. The data made it impossible to assess the classroom effects of social class composition nearly as well as at the school level, so the validity of the classroom racial composition effect was uncertain. In addition, the report explored the relation between desegregation and racial attitudes associated with desegregation: interracial tension often was higher in more integrated schools, and interracial contact often was little greater in biracial than in segregated schools. Desegregated schools seemed as likely to produce tension and conflict as understanding and interracial harmony.

There ensued many smaller studies of particular districts as desegregation accelerated, but these accumulated the same small and inconsistent differences.[16] None of this helped settle the question of what school desegregation was good for. If it didn't consistently or appreciably improve things for black students, awkward questions arose about its value—particularly in light of earlier findings that segregation damaged the minds and future opportunities of Negro youth. These queries might have lain mercifully quiet in academic groves and bureaucratic files, had it not been for the fact that research only reflected experience. Desegregated schools turned out to be more uncomfortable than anyone had expected, and often they were downright dangerous. Racism, it seemed, could no more be avoided in desegregated schools than in segregated ones. This rather stimulated second thoughts all around, inviting blacks to reflect on the comforts and advantages of separate institutions. By the close of the last decade, several black researchers argued that the problem was as much racist and discriminatory desegregation schemes as it was segregation.[17]

If research helped to redefine the problem of segregation, the process was reinforced by social and political trends. Population shifts produced an increasing number of central cities with heavy black majorities in the public schools. Some social scientists interpreted this as evidence that racial balance was impossible within central city schools. They maintained that desegregation would therefore have to occur on a metropolitan scale. They tried to support this with evidence that the academic effects of integration disappeared in majority-black settings, and with research on the success of small-scale city-suburban busing programs.[18]

But the notion was not warmly received. Black politicians in these central cities, especially those with an interest in the mayor's offices, quickly developed an allergy to anything that would unsettle white or disperse black support. The mere mention of metropolitan school desegregation is well calculated to do both. And some social scientists took exception to the idea that desegregation required the dilution of black student bodies in mostly white settings: by the 1970's, that approach struck many as a sort of *raffiné* racism.[19] Other researchers wondered whether the social costs of metropolitan desegregation in cities like Detroit would outweigh the benefits.[20] Their uncertainty on this point was not eased by ambiguous findings on the academic impact of desegregation.

These reservations were reinforced by the movement for black community control. Somehow the conjunction of Negro demands for self-government with white proposals for metropolitan dispersal of black students seemed odd, if not downright embarrassing. Increasingly, social scientists held that the central problem in matters of education and race was no longer segregation; rather they argued that the racism that had engendered segregation also made desegregation a demeaning and humiliating experience for blacks. Desegregation had come to seem as much a problem as segregation.

This brief account hardly captures all the ways in which ideas about the problems of schools and race have changed. But the central point is that early and relatively clear definitions of the problem have tended to blur and disintegrate under the pressure of experience. Once upon a time the problem was legally mandated dual schools, but by 1970—not to mention the later years of Boston and Detroit—that seemed almost quaint.

Our account suggests that this phenomenon occurred in several ways. For one thing, segregation turned out to be more complex than had been expected: in 1954 no one really thought school desegregation suits would turn out to reach school flagpoles, teachers' rooms, and student clubs. For another, at the beginning of efforts to solve social problems, there is almost always a preferred solution, a social device of some sort that is appealing precisely because it offers a simplified view of how things can be improved. "Disestablishing the racially dual school system" was precisely such a device, but it turned out to hide a swamp of complexities. Although it could be given a reasonably clear meaning in many southern school districts, its import was much less clear in majority black rural counties in Mississippi, in the central cities of Atlanta or Memphis, or in such northern cities as Detroit or Boston.

And last but not least, the segregation problem became less clear because social reality changed. Sometimes the changes were unrelated to desegregation: i.e., population shifts in central cities are a century-long trend, and they gradually frustrated efforts to desegregate schools. As a result, what had been a complex problem involving single jurisdictions became, willy-nilly, a supercomplicated problem crossing jurisdictional lines within metropolitan areas. But sometimes the changes in social reality were the direct result of efforts to integrate schools. For example, events beginning with *Brown* tended to legitimize Negro grievances, to encourage their expression, and to focus attention on them. Because it seemed that the problem might be solved after all, and because it seemed that grievances long contained could really be expressed, blacks began to ventilate feelings they had long kept from the world, or from themselves. One result of the school desegregation process following from *Brown* was that blacks developed a much more refined sense of racial injustice in schools, a much decreased willingness to stand the pain, and a sharply reduced appetite for white people's solutions. All of this worked a change in social reality: what would have been an entirely acceptable integrated high school in 1954 would have seemed an outrageous insult in 1974.

So, trying to solve a social problem changes the way the problem is seen; it complicates and diversifies views of the problem; it makes once-appealing solutions seem limited; and it suggests alternative solutions. The result is not just that the problem comes to seem more complex, but also that in some ways it comes to seem different and contradictory. The current view that desegregation is a major social problem is at cross purposes with many ideas surrounding the *Brown* decision.

This story suggests that research plays several roles in all this. For one thing, research on social policy constitutes a form of reporting to society—researchers are part of the intelligence apparatus by which society learns what seems to be happening.[21] Research and evaluation were among the vehicles by which Americans learned about the ambiguous impact of integration on achievement, about its contradictory effect on attitudes, and about the perils of the desegregation process. In this role, research may seem a relatively passive instrument, but the opportunities for selection and interpretation of evidence belie this. What is reported to society profoundly influences what society learns.[22]

Second, social problem research often plays a critical role, picking apart earlier ideas and assumptions. The Coleman Report, for example, used powerful statistical techniques to analyze the impact of desegregation on achievement. Quite unintentionally, it blew apart many established ideas about schools and race. The intent was not critical, but the effect was to raise basic questions about the effects of desegregation. And third, research and social commentary by researchers often turn out to be a way of expressing new social tendencies and intellectual currents. Much of the "research" associated with the movement for community control partook of this quality. It brought new ideas into main research currents, provided new fodder for the academic herds, and helped to legitimize new ideas by introducing them in scientific garb.

Thus research sometimes reports a complicating reality, and sometimes it complicates our picture of reality through criticisms and the introduction of new ideas. In both ways it helps to make our understanding of social problems more complex. And because formal inquiry is somewhat less absent-minded than the daily media, it provides an historical record of these changes for researchers and research consumers. This only heightens the sense of complexity and change. Research usually is not the primary moving force in all this, but because of the growing importance of formal studies in social reportage, it is rarely unimportant. In one way or another, it is a significant force in redefining and complicating our views of social problems.

Research Methods and Frameworks

One might think from the account so far that social problems, not research, are to blame: the problems sneak up on the unwary investigator slowly, seductively let down their veils, and reveal their alluring complexity. The hopeful and innocent analyst is both captivated and befuddled. But research contributes its share to befuddlement, something that is most evident in considering the effects of improved research on the clarity of findings.

Two improvements are central. One embraces the remarkable methodological and technical advances in the social sciences of the last few decades. As a result of computer technology and the avalanche of money for large-scale studies, researchers can now collect evidence on many factors in any social situation. At the same time, methodologists and data analysts have adapted and developed statistical techniques that permit analysis of many such factors at one time. Because these techniques permit assessment of the relative importance of various causal influences, social scientists can now attack social phenomena with much more finesse than was possible three decades ago.

All of this encouraged the collection of much more diverse and representative data. Social scientists have known about the importance of sampling for some time, but it took advances in data management, analysis, and financial support to translate these canons of design into a program for action. As a result, investigators can not only report findings that are statistically more credible for national policy, but they can consider all sorts of interesting sub-groups: they can weigh regional differences; they can explore urban-rural variations; or they can peer into bedroom suburbs. And finally, research has become a more self-conscious process: the growth of the enterprise and its increasing technical refinements have heightened awareness of problems of analysis, methodology, and design. Methodology and research criticism has become a central interest in the social sciences, and a focus in most debates over policy research.[23]

A second improvement is the diversification of desegregation research since the early 1950's. At the outset, most investigations were psychological, but gradually psychology lost its corner on the market. Economists, sociologists, and anthropologists have been drawn in, as have researchers from the professions—notably education and law. The relative importance of psychological research has diminished. Research on race and schools is thus not only more refined methodologically, but it has flowered under the influence of several different disciplinary and professional orientations.

These advances are good for research, but one reward for the better studies has been a clearer idea of just how muddy the waters really are. Research on the effects of segregation and desegregation reveals this nicely. It began with the Clarks' psychological studies of racial awareness and self-esteem.[24] That work, and the research summarized in the Social Science Brief, supported the idea that segregation caused psychological damage to Negro children. This broadly psychological emphasis was given specific focus by two developments of the 1950's. One was research by such *eminences* as Garrett and Shuey; they maintained that, although desegregation would never improve the achievement of Negro students because of their inherited intellectual inferiority, the achievement of white students would be impaired by the classroom presence of this foreign, academically leaden black mass.[25] In the political atmosphere of massive resistance and interposition, some social scientists felt it was essential to answer these attacks, and show that integration did improve achievement. They argued that desegregation raised Negro achievement and IQ test scores, and tried in their research to prove the point.[26] This tendency was given added force by the post-Sputnik pressure for better achievement, and by the growing fashion of programs to improve the academic performance of "culturally deprived" students.

The result was to ensconce achievement test scores as the variable of chief interest in research on race and schools between *Brown* and the middle 1960's. At the outset, these studies were few in number and straightforward in design; the relation between schools' racial composition and test scores would be presented in simple one- or two-way tables. In some cases it seemed as though black students were better off in desegregated schools and in some cases it did not.[27] But the results were easy to read, and they dealt in a currency everyone thought they understood.

The Coleman Report, published in July 1966, changed all that, for it brought a formidable array of methodological refinements to bear on the question. The Report was based on a nationally representative sample of schools, and was designed to permit complex multiple regression analyses of the relative impact of racial composition, school resources, student background, and school social class composition on achievement and attitudes. In these analyses, schools' racial composition was found to have no significant independent association with student achievement. This was as much of a surprise to Coleman and his co-authors as to anyone else;[28] the assumptions of an entire generation of research were dissolved in Section III of the Report.

But although findings fail, methodology marched on. The Coleman Report was equally stunning for its conclusion that there was little relation between school resources and school achievement, and the two issues tended to merge after the Report's publication. The Coleman Report was attacked almost as soon as it hit the streets, initially by Levin and Bowles. They took Coleman to task for a series of high methodological crimes:[29] the Report, they argued, had used the wrong regression statistics; it was flawed by problems of non-response; it used analytic techniques that incorrectly understated the impact of school resources; it was therefore useless for policy guidance. Levin and Bowles produced an impressive array of methodological arguments against the Report's results, and they marshalled other arguments for findings the Report had not found. Their essay certainly somewhat undermined the Report's credibility.

The episode also nicely illustrated disciplinary differences in the use of analytic techniques. Coleman was a sociologist, and used the regression statistic dearest to that discipline (the standardized beta coefficient, which reflects the relative importance of several forces in a complex system of relationships). Bowles and Levin were economists, and they held out for another regression statistic, which reflects the unique impact of one variable in an input-output system (the unstandardized beta coefficient). Adding disciplines to the scientific fray sharpened issues and created new arguments.[30]

Reading the Report analysis was hard enough, but umpiring debates over the correct regression statistic taxed the brains of even rather sophisticated researchers. And the story grew no simpler. In the aftermath of Coleman, the Civil Rights Commission produced its reanalysis of his data, and this further complicated things because of curiosities arising from the Report's nationally representative character. The findings about classroom integration in *Racial Isolation* were based on data from high schools in the northeastern urban United States. There did seem to be an effect of integration in this region. But the Commission also published an appendix volume, wherein lay parallel analyses of classroom integration from other regions. Some results seemed to support those for the urban northeast, but others did not. Sometimes they showed no positive impact of integrated classrooms, and sometimes they showed a negative impact. The Commission's researchers made little of this in their report. This was partly because there were fewer integrated high schools outside the northeast, but partly because the findings were at odds with those in the main report. But in any event, having nationally-representative data did not produce more definitive conclusions.

Later in the decade, reanalyses of the Coleman Report data became a growth industry, supported by government grants, public-spirited foundations, and scholarly animosity. One group at Harvard, under the scientific leadership of Daniel P. Moynihan, produced a raft of refinements and further qualifications.[31] David Armor, for example, found that school integration helped black students, but only if they were in more than token integrated, but less than majority black, schools. Whites, it seemed, were good for blacks if taken in medium doses, rather than in very small or very large ones. Economic contributors in Moynihan's volume continued to moan over the Report and attack its results, whereas Jencks and other sociologists upheld the statistical virtue of Coleman's original findings with new and better analytic techniques. Another reanalysis group at the U.S. Office of Education attacked Coleman's and Jencks' findings on school effects while repelling the advances of Levin, Bowles, Kain, and Hanushek on the Report's methodology.[32] As one would expect from an agency that spends most of its time giving away money to public schools, the Office of Education group found that school resources did make a difference.

The reanalyses continued for years, producing more questions, more qualifications, and more occasions to exercise new analytic muscles. Some researchers thought Coleman had overstated the impact of social-class integration.[33] Others, reanalyzing the Civil Rights Commission's work, found that the effects of classroom integration seemed to hold at the ninth grade but not at the twelfth grade.[34] Jencks and company, in *Inequality*, thought there might be a small effect of school racial mixing in elementary schools, but they emphasized the modesty of the effect and the uncertainty of the evidence.[35] Shortly thereafter, the Civil Rights Commission re-entered the picture, this time denouncing the inadequacy of previous research on the subject, and proclaiming its unreliability for policy guidance. The Commission called for a more comprehensive, complex, longitudinal study to resolve the issues.[36] The reanalyses, then, produced a swarm of contrary ideas, a host of refined analytic techniques, and a growing despair over the prospects for clear conclusions on the issues.

The controversies continue, however. They have moved on from what now seem old-hat simple multiple regression techniques to such new and more complex analytic methods as path analysis, multi-stage regression, and the like. They also have moved to new and more complex analytic issues (the effects of schooling on adult success, rather than just on achievement).[37] And they have moved on to new bodies of data, the Coleman Report having been rubbed raw in the scientific fray.[38] The effect of racial composition of schools on students occasionally appears in these super-sophisticated combats in mathematical sociology and econometrics, but the issue seems to have been dwarfed by larger questions about whether schooling itself makes a difference, and to have been obscured by the proliferation of complex analytic techniques. More employment for more sophisticated sociologists and economists has been found, but the effects of school desegregation now dance through all this like a will-o-the-wisp, appearing in some studies and under some conditions and not appearing in others. The only conclusions on which most researchers now seem to agree is that the data collected in the 1960's are inadequate. More sophisticated analytic techniques uncovered many previously undiscovered defects in the evidence, and thus revealed the need for more research and better data. Science marches on.

Our story of the improvement in desegregation research does not end here. As research on test scores accumulated, so did questions about the approach to assessing school integration. The concentration on test scores began to seem myopic to many social scientists who had no quarrel with advanced methodologies.[39] One reason for this was that some researchers became uneasy about the persistent unrelieved black-white gap in achievement scores, a gap that seemed unresponsive to anything from integration to school improvement programs. Another reason was the fact that, by the middle and late 1960's, sociology and economics had entered research on education and race in force. These disciplines saw the work differently from psychology, and they contemplated other outcomes of desegregation. And finally, the more research that was done on test scores, the more psychologists began to question the meaning of the tests.

These developments led some researchers to question the technical basis of the tests: they argued that the instruments were so constructed as to minimize the influence of any school-to-school variation, whether in resources or in racial composition.[40] It led other researchers to question the cultural foundation of the tests; they argued that, because the tests were standardized on middle-class whites, they were biased against the poor and members of minority groups.[41] On both counts, the credibility of tests suffered. The more research that was done, the less clear it seemed that test scores were a sensible way to assess the impact of integration. Once again, as research plumbed the issues further, complexity grew and the evidence seemed less amenable to clear policy advice.

A second result of these struggles over test scores was to encourage studies on other outcomes of desegregation. Increasingly, researchers noted that desegregation was supposed to have something to do with hearts as well as minds—with interracial attitudes and behavior as well as test scores.[42] They cautioned that excessive reliance on tests would produce a distorted picture. As more and more attention was focused on the social-psychological impact of desegregation, research on interracial attitudes and behavior prospered. The sophistication of studies in this area increased appreciably but, as in the case of test scores, these improvements did nothing to clarify things.

Early research on racial attitudes was dominated by Gordon Allport's and Samuel Stouffer's work in the 1940's and early 1950's.[43] These studies seemed to show that racial attitudes would benefit from interracial contact in equal status situations. These studies, like other less-well-known efforts of the period, viewed racial attitudes as a self-evidently important outcome of biracial settings. One reason for this was that social psychologists assumed that the links between attitudes and behavior were close. Another was that, in a period when bigoted attitudes were widely and openly expressed, liberal social scientists understandably regarded the reduction of such expression as a good in itself. Given the verbal and psychological brutalities of a Jim Crow society, harmonious interracial attitudes seemed self-evidently important.

But one consequence of increased attention to the impact of desegregation on interracial attitudes was increased dissatisfaction with existing attitude measures. They were few in number; they needed technical improvement; and, as desegregation spread, the available sorts of interracial situations grew, demanding new measures appropriate to the circumstances. Measures thus proliferated, and by the late 1960's the harvest included a rich growth: forced choice questionnaire items, social distance scales, measures of racial stereotyping, doll choice measures, sociometric preferences, simple Likert scales, and semantic differentials.[44]

The improvements here are plain. Attitudes are not simple, and it makes perfect sense to pursue them in a variety of ways. In addition, situations vary; sociometric choices, for example, make more sense in a third-grade classroom than does a thirty-item questionnaire about racial attitudes. But the advantages were not unalloyed. One problem was that studies seldom repeated the measures, let alone replicated the study conditions. Sometimes the issues were a little different, sometimes the populations varied, and almost always the measures were different. This did not seem to be a serious problem until researchers began to notice the tendency of attitude measures to be weakly related. Even within studies, there were almost always low correlations between scales measuring interracial attitudes.[45] If different ways of measuring the same conceptual variable did not lead to the same conclusions, then the proliferation of measures created clear problems of generalizability. Consequently, most studies stood as socially scientific islands, each more or less gleaming but most somewhat incomparable to the others.

The few replications of earlier reserarch further unsettled the issues. For example, Judith Porter's replication of Kenneth and Mamie Clark's original doll play studies turned up findings about the racial preferences and self-esteem of young black children that were often different from, and sometimes at odds with, the earlier research.[46] Some of this might be explained by problems with the measures, or with their application to particular populations, as Porter suggested. The fact was, however, that one consequence of improved measurement was more uncertainty about the measures and what they were measuring.

A second problem arose partly from evidence about the weak relationships among measures. This increased the uncertainty about the validity of any single measure, and made it seem ever more sensible to use more measures. But the focus of most work of this sort was demonstrating and explaining the causal relationship between interracial schools and racial attitudes. And the weak connections among measures meant that explaining the causal connection between biracial schools and one measure of racial attitudes need not necessarily hold for explaining the connection for another measure. Interracial schools that seemed to produce a good racial climate based on a self-administered questionnaire seemed to produce a bigoted climate based on observers' reports.[47] This confused interpretations of the relation between racial attitudes and interracial settings. Nor did it do much to boost confidence in the measures. Researchers learned that the way they measured attitudes seemed to influence the sort of attitudes they "found." Although self-consciousness about biases introduced in these ways works to improve research methodology, it does not produce much clarity about policy implications, nor does it build confidence in the solidity of research findings.

Another key development in the last ten or fifteen years' research on attitudes concerned behavior. Social psychologists who had focused research on attitudes had, of course, assumed that a change in attitudes would lead to a change in behavior. But by the mid-1960's, social psychology had changed its tune. As one reviewer concluded:

> Most socially significant questions involve overt behavior rather than peoples' feelings, and the assumption that feelings are directly translated into action has not been demonstrated.[48]

This shift had important implications for the study of racial attitudes in schools. The "socially significant questions" about desegregation clearly went beyond the reduction of verbal expressions of racial prejudice. Researchers were concerned with interracial behavior—usually with friendships between black and white students, but also with other aspects of life in desegregated schools (interracial violence, communication, dating, etc.). It therefore became important to understand the relationship between racial attitudes and interracial behavior.

The research into the attitude-behavior link showed that the link was fragile. In some instances there were insignificant associations between the two, and in other cases the relationship was reversed. In one study of biracial groups, white students from integrated schools were more likely to dominate blacks than were whites from all-white schools.[49] In another study, white college students who expressed more prejudice actually took more suggestions from blacks in group tasks than did white students who expressed less prejudice.[50] It is easy to conjure up after-the-fact explanations for such findings, but that is a little off the point. The advance of research on racial attitudes has revealed no strong or consistent connection between attitudes and behavior. This is an interesting and important research development. But it rather weakened the ground under an entire line of policy-relevant studies based exclusively on attitude research.

Partly as a consequence of these findings, measures of behavior or reports of behavior came to be included routinely in research on desegregated schools. Researchers no longer depended exclusively on student attitudes to measure racial climates, but asked for reports of interracial behavior as well. In fact, the Coleman Report asked students only one question about the racial climate of their schools, and that one was behavioral—a report of cross-racial friendship patterns. Adding behavioral reports to attitude measures created a whole new set of outcomes to explain, greatly complicating the job of understanding the effect of school factors on student outcomes. And substituting behavioral for attitudinal variables—as many researchers did—made later studies increasingly incompatible with earlier findings.

In an effort to sort out the hodge-podge of findings, social scientists turned their attention to the social circumstances that might mediate the effects of interracial situations on attitudes and behavior. They turned up a formidable list of considerations. In some research they weighed the impact of teachers' and principals' racial attitudes. In other cases they asked whether segregation or integration of classrooms made a difference. In some others they probed whether the social and economic class of students—or the mixture of class backgrounds—affected student reactions to desegregation. And still other studies explored a growing list of other influences: length of students' experience in interracial schools; the extent of minority students' participation in extracurricular activities; the age or grade level of students; community attitudes; and the degree of internal tracking and grouping.[51]

This is quite a list of influences. For each one there was at least one study that claimed that the factor in question did mediate the relationship between the influence of interracial settings and racial attitudes on behavior. But often some other study presented contrary findings; factors that seemed important in some studies seemed unimportant in others. Ordinarily it was not possible to know just why this was so. In some cases the measures of racial harmony varied from study to study; in other cases the measures of attitudes or situational influences varied as well. Finally, the times of the research and the local circumstances also varied. As a result, the findings seemed unstable, and little was learned about the relative salience of the situational influences on racial climate. One study did try to quantify variables to compare their relative importance, but it did not bring much greater clarity.[52] Some situational influences had no impact on the racial attitudes measured; some had very weak effects; and in some cases the effects varied between different attitude and behavioral measures. It is not clear whether this mixed assortment of results should be blamed on the quantification of subtle social phenomena, on the cross-sectional character of the study, or on some more substantive considerations. Complicated multivariate analyses of situational factors that mediate the impact of racial composition of schools on student attitudes and behavior suggested just how complex the process might be. But it did little to clear up the contradictions of earlier studies, or to offer much guidance for policy.

Indeed, technical and methodological refinements only confused the meaning of earlier studies. The most recent research review concluded that, for the most part, "these studies are in no sense comparable with each other."[53] The research has grown, and grown more sophisticated, but the findings have not been cumulative. A good part of the reason is that there is no strong theory that suggested what influences should be observed, or what outcome variables are most important. Given this situation, social science tends to proliferate under the influence of empirical ideas, weak theories, intuitions from practical experience, suggestions from other fields, or the analytic possibilities suggested by new methodologies. Under such conditions, scientific improvement is a term with a somewhat special—and often purely technical—meaning. The fruit of such scientific developments is sometimes rich and always varied, but not necessarily very coherent.

Thus, if social-psychological research was a useful balance to the earlier reliance on test scores, it did not exactly clarify matters. In fact, simply by adding another disciplinary perspective on desegregation, it complicated the total picture. This phenomenon reappeared in the late 1960's and early 1970's, as sociologists and economists entered the field, and was most striking in the work of some anthropologically oriented social scientists. They rejected all forms of quantitative and survey research, and undertook direct observational studies of desegregated schools. They argued that more traditional approaches were bound to produce a distorted picture, and their results certainly were consistent with these ideas. Not only did these ethnographies offer a different disciplinary approach to the study of schools and race, but they presented rather a different picture of desegregation. They found social segregation within schools, insensitivity and racial stereotyping on the part of teachers, defensiveness and denial by teachers and administrators, and a mixed and often unhappy experience for black children.

A recent effort, for example, reported on a desegregation program carried out in a way that most communities would probably regard as either quite acceptable or ideal.[54] But it seemed a demeaning and unhappy experience for most of the black children involved, although none of the school staff appears to have known this. This was rather a different portrait than emerged from the various quantitative evaluations of desegregation, and it resulted in rather more astringent conclusions. The author, an integrationist, held that desegregation simply ought not occur under such conditions.

In summary, then, the improvement of research has had paradoxical results. On one hand we have a less simple-minded and more plausible account of social reality. Artifacts are reduced, distortions due to faulty method are often eliminated, overblown interpretations are corrected, and more careful analyses are presented. The technical sophistication of recent research on desegregation is such as to inspire more confidence than twenty years ago that the results of any given study are valid. But these changes have led to more studies that disagree, to more qualified conclusions, more arguments, and more arcane reports and unintelligible results. If any given study is more valid, the inferences to policy from the lot seem much more uncertain.

One reason for this, as we have pointed out, is that methodological refinement in social research often is not convergent, but rather tends to sharpen differences. Another is that the progress of research on a social problem tends to draw in different disciplines and professions. These involve diverse research traditions, and the consequence is more differences in approach and interpretation. And still another reason is that the progress of research on social problems tends to move backward, from relatively simple ideas about problems and their solutions to ever more basic questions about both. The net result is a more varied picture of reality, but such results do not lend themselves to straightforward policy guidance.

Conclusions

One thing is clear from this story. The more research on a social problem prospers, the harder it is for policy-makers and courts to get the sort of guidance they often say they want: clear recommendations about what to do, or at least clear alternatives. Predictably, the result is frustration. In both the race and school finance cases, for example, one can see the judges becoming more exasperated with the complexities and contradictions of research.[55]

We expect that courts, like most other customers at the social science supermarket, can expect no relief. Most litigants in school cases will be able to find some scientific support for their views, and many judges will try valiantly to decide which is right. Others, viewing the proliferation of contending scientific alternatives, will cast a Skelly Wright-ish pox on all their houses.[56] Both courses of action seem understandable. After all, courts have cases to decide, and with some exceptions social science is not at its best in giving clear advice about exactly what to in a single case.

But although we expect continual frustration in this connection, we do not think that social science is irrelevant to social policy, nor do we think it should be. At its best, social research provides a reasonable sense of the various ways a problem can be understood, and a reasonable account of how solutions might be approached. Such general advice about controversial and problematic issues is a useful contribution of social knowledge, even if it is not crisply relevant to particular decisions. Unfortunately, although it can sometimes be introduced into a court record by way of the adversary process, often that process would probably exclude or distort such advice.

If this is right, it does not explain exactly how we should think about research and its relation to policy. One alternative is to regard research on social policy as a moveable and slowly expanding feast. As research prospers, the chances grow that potential consumers will find something to satisfy their particular tastes. Thus, if one thinks of policy formation as a process of competition for values and social goods, one can think of research as ammunition for the various parties at interest.[57] The growing diversity of approaches and findings may frustrate any given user of research, but the net satisfaction of all users will increase as more of them find studies that suit their special purposes. It goes almost without saying that this view will seem satisfying in proportion to the fairness of the competition. If some viewpoints or interests are chronically over-represented and others routinely neglected by research, the social science smorgasbord will fatten some while others starve.[58]

Certainly this picture seems plausible in light of our discussion. The last twenty years have seen not only the prosperity of research on race and schools, but also the more extensive involvement of research on all sides of complex judicial, executive, and legislative issues.

But if it is plausible, the picture is not complete. It rather suggests that social science is a purely adversarial instrument. Our account, however, suggests that the improvement of research has not simply been a matter of sharper argumentation. In addition, we know more. Research has helped provide a better picture of the desegregation process; it has taught us something about how desegregation does and does not work, and why; and it has helped broaden our picture of who desegregation affects. Typically, however, these improvements do not offer a handy solution. Indeed, among the things we can learn from the accumulated studies of the last few decades are cautions: about easy solutions, simple formulations, and social science findings.

On this view, then, research on a social problem might be portrayed as a contribution to social wisdom. As more is learned through experience and investigation, simpler and appealing ideas give away to more qualified advice. Certainly support can be found for this view as well; courts and executive agencies have learned something about the complexities of the desegregation process, and in part they have learned from research. In some cases they even have tried to put this learning into practice. The lessons may seem general and cautious, but nonetheless they represent a sort of policy guidance.

Finally, the studies recited in this essay suggest that research is part and parcel of social enthusiasms. When whipping up the brains of America's youth was in fashion in the late 1950's and early 1960's, research on race and schools stepped to the tune of test scores. When desegregation was Out and community control was In, fate-control was all the rage. And when school desegregation came North early in the 1970's, many liberal and moderate northern politicians who had supported this reform in the South suddenly broke and ran. Research on race and schools suffered a similar affliction, evident in Coleman's announcement that compulsory desegregation is chasing white people from the nation's central cities.[59]

On this view, research and policy might be pictured as partners in social change: as different social enthusiasms come into fashion, research and policy embrace and express them. Research contributes something to these changing climates of opinion, but it also responds to broader shifts in social belief and expression. Research and policy affect each other in these affairs, but often they seem to float together on the surface of larger waves.

These three pictures of the relation between research and policy imply rather different criteria for evaluating the contribution of research. If we think of the social science smorgasbord, it seems important to make sure that all the important dishes are present, and all the diners fed. We would evaluate the quality of desegregation research at least partly in terms of fairness, both in the feast laid on and in its consumption. If, alternatively, we think of research as an incremental growth in social wisdom, then we would evaluate it in terms of its contribution to such insightful guidance. And if we imagine policy and research both to be swept away on waves of social enthusiasm, we might retreat, puzzled at the difficulty of devising any evaluative criterion.

Regardless of which picture is most appealing, our account suggests that on the evaluative criterion advanced by most advocates of policy research—does the research contribute more precise guidance for particular decisions?—most research would fail miserably. But we think the reason for this lies not so much with the quality of research as with a misconception of the research process. In more cases than not, more precise guidance for particular decisions is a dream hopelessly at variance with the divergent and pluralistic character of social policy research. Rather than helping, the dream generally seems to distract research workers from a clear view of their work and its role.

One other thing that the three accounts of the relation between research and policy share is agnosticism about whether research on policy issues is convergent. This is helpful because, as we said at the outset, the evidence on this point is shaky. In fact, we think it is most useful to picture the research process as a dialogue about social reality, an historical conversation about social problems and how they might be solved. A dialogue is good to the extent that the various relevant views are present, and to the extent that points of difference are clarified. A dialogue is good to the extent that the whole represents a satisfying, if necessarily diverse, account of the ways in which an issue can be framed, explored, and resolved. We think social research is best conceived as such a dialogue—rather than as a problem-solving exercise—and have tried to show how, as research prospers, the conversation is enriched.

This is not to suggest that the progress of research on race and schools has been entirely satisfying, for some parties have been better represented at the social science smorgasbord than others. Nor is it to suggest that truth will complaisantly out. Dialogues, after all, are subject to fashion changes; and although they can produce what we think of as wisdom, it often is only a passing agreement that later comes unstrung. Nor would we say that there have been no distractions, or foolish expenditures on research frippery. But clearly the conversation has grown more rich. Our chief point, however, is that it is helpful to see social research this way. To those who ply the trade, it offers a more sensible view of their work; among those who would like guidance, it presents a basis for more reasonable expectations. It also helps explain why improved knowledge does not always lead to more effective action.

Notes

[1] See, for example, the citations in Nancy H. St. John, *School Desegregation* (New York: John Wiley & Sons, 1975).

[2] Pettigrew and Rose give examples of this from their personal experiences. See Thomas F. Pettigrew, Sociological consulting in race relations, 6 *American Sociologist* 44-47 (1971); Arnold Rose, The social scientist as an expert witness in court cases, in P. Lazarsfeld, W. Sewell, and H. Wilensky, *The Uses of Sociology* (New York: Basic Books, 1967).

[3] D. J. Armor, The evidence on busing, 28 *The Public Interest* 90-126 (1972); T. F. Pettigrew, E. L. Useem, C. Normand, and M. S. Smith, Busing: a review of "the evidence," 30 *The Public Interest* 88-118 (1973); D. J. Armor, The double double standard: a reply, 30 *The Public Interest* 119-131 (1973).

[4] James S. Coleman *et al.*, *Trends in School Segregation* (Washington, D.C.: The Urban Institute, August 1975); Reynolds Farley, "School Integration and White Flight," paper presented at the Symposium on School Desegregation and White Flight, Brookings Institution, Washington, D.C., August 15, 1975.

[5] James S. Coleman *et al.*, *Equality of Educational Opportunity* (Washington, D.C.: U.S. Government Printing Office, 1966).

[6] Christopher Jencks *et al.*, *Inequality* (New York: Harper & Row, 1972); Marshall S. Smith, Equality of Educational Opportunity: the basic findings reconsidered, in Frederick Mosteller and Daniel P. Moynihan (eds.), *On Equality of Educational*

Opportunity (New York: Random House, 1972); Armor, The evidence on busing; Pettigrew *et al.*, Busing: a review; Coleman *et al.*, *Equality of Educational Opportunity*.

[7]Frank Lewis and Frank Zarb, Federal program evaluation from the OMB perspective, 34 *Public Administration Review* 308-317 (1974); Eliot Richardson, *Responsibility and Responsiveness* (Washington, D.C.: U.S. Department of Health, Education, and Welfare, 1972).

[8]See, for example, James S. Coleman, *Policy Research in the Social Sciences* (Morristown: General Learning Press, 1972); Daniel P. Moynihan, *Maximum Feasible Misunderstanding* (New York: Free Press, 1969); Walter Williams, *Social Policy Research and Analysis* (New York: American Elsevier, 1971); Robert Scott and Arnold Shore, Sociology and policy analysis, 9 *American Sociologist* 51 (1974).

[9]For a discussion of these points, see Thomas Kuhn, *The Structure of Scientific Revolutions* (Chicago: University of Chicago Press, 1962).

[10]Social Science Brief (Appendix to Appellant's Briefs: The Effects of Segregation and the Consequences of Desegregation: A Social Science Statement); reprinted in Kenneth B. Clark, *Prejudice and Your Child*, 2nd edition (Boston: Beacon Press, 1963), pp. 166-181.

[11]Henry E. Garrett, A note on the intelligence scores of negroes and whites in 1918, 40 *Journal of Abnormal and Social Psychology* 344-346 (1945); Henry E. Garrett, The equalitarian dogma, 1 *Mankind Quarterly* 253 (1961); Audrey Shuey, *The Testing of Negro Intelligence* (Lynchburg, Va.: Bell, 1958).

[12]See the extensive reviews in St. John, *School Desegregation*, and in Meyer Weinberg, The relationship between school desegregation and academic achievement: a review of the research, 39 *Law and Contemporary Problems* 240-270. (1975).

[13]Coleman *et al.*, *Equality of Educational Opportunity*.

[14]See, for example, U.S. Commission on Civil Rights, *Racial Isolation in the Public Schools* (Washington, D.C.: U.S. Government Printing Office, 1967), vols. 1 & 2.

[15]*Ibid.*

[16]For example, St. John writes, "In sum, comparative studies of the racial attitudes of segregated and desegregated school children are inconclusive. Findings are inconsistent and mixed regardless of whether students' racial attitudes or friendship choice was the object of the study, regardless of whether desegregation was by neighborhood or busing, voluntary or mandatory, and regardless of whether the study design was cross-sectional or longitudinal." *School Desegregation*, p. 80.

[17]See, for example, Charles V. Hamilton, Race and education: a search for legitimacy, 38 *Harvard Educational Review* 669-684 (1968).

[18]The 1967 USCCR report was the first in this line of thought.

[19]Derrick A. Bell, Jr., Waiting on the promise of *Brown*, 39 *Law and Contemporary Problems* 341-373 (1975).

[20]For example, Nathan Glazer writes: "If, then, the judges are moving toward a reorganization of American education because they believe this will improve relations between the races, they are acting neither on evidence nor on experience but on faith. And in so acting on faith they are pushing against many legitimate

interests: the interest in using tax money for education rather than transportation; the interest of the working and lower middle classes in attending schools near their homes; the interest of all groups, including black groups, in developing some measure of control over the institutions which affect their lives; the interest of all people in retaining freedom of choice wherever this is possible." See N. Glazer, Is busing necessary?, 53 *Commentary* 39-52 (March 1972).

[21] For an expansion of this point, see David K. Cohen, "Reporting to Society," unpublished ms., Harvard University.

[22] For example, Henry Levin has pointed out this phenomenon in the case of school expenditures. "Presentation of evidence on the relationship between educational expenditures and cognitive achievement implicitly narrows the context within which the effects of using expenditure patterns will be considered. While the two sides to this debate disagree on the effects of school resources, both have accepted the view that standardized achievement scores are the appropriate focus for exploring educational outcomes." See H. M. Levin, "Education, life chances, and the courts: the role of social science evidence, 39 *Law and Contemporary Problems* 237 (1975).

[23] As one of many examples, see Donald T. Campbell, Assessing the impact of planned social change, in G. Lyons (ed.), *Social Research and Policies* (Hanover: University Press of New England, 1975), pp. 3-45.

[24] Kenneth and Mamie Clark, Racial identification and preference in Negro children, in T. Newcomb and E. Hartley (eds.), *Readings in Social Psychology*, 1st edition (New York: Holt and Co., 1947).

[25] Garrett, The equalitarian dogma; Shuey, *The Testing of Negro Intelligence.*

[26] For example, Thomas Pettigrew writes about the desegregation of the Washington, D.C., schools: "Though Negro students, swelled by migrants, now comprised three fourths of the student body, achievement test scores had risen significantly for each grade level sampled and each subject area tested approached or equalled national norms. Furthermore, both Negro and White students shared in these increments." See T. F. Pettigrew, *A Profile of the Negro American* (Princeton: D. Van Nostrand Co., 1964), p. 128.

[27] For a discussion of these studies, see Sheldon White *et al.*, *Federal Programs for Young Children, Vol. 2: Review of Evaluation Data for Federally Sponsored Projects for Children*, Appendix 11 A (Washington, D.C.: U.S. Govt. Printing Office, 1973); also, Robert A. Mathai, "The Academic Performance of Negro Students: An Analysis of the Research Findings from Several Busing Programs," Special Qualifying Paper, Harvard University Graduate School of Education, June 1968. One example of such studies is the report on the effects of desegregation in Berkeley, California. See Neil Sullivan, The Berkeley experience, 38 *Harvard Educational Review* 148-155 (1968).

[28] See Gerald Paul Grant, "The politics of the Coleman Report," unpublished Dissertation, Harvard University Graduate School of Education, 1972.

[29] Samuel Bowles and Henry M. Levin, The determinants of scholastic achievement—an appraisal of some recent evidence, 3 *Journal of Human Resources* 3-24 (1968).

[30] For fuller treatments of this phenomenon, see James S. Coleman, Integration of sociology and the other social sciences through policy analysis, in James C.

Charlesworth (ed.), *Integration of the Social Sciences* (Philadelphia: American Academy of Political and Social Science, 1972), Monograph 14; and David K. Cohen and Michael S. Garet, Reforming educational policy with applied social research, 45 *Harvard Educational Review* 17-43 (1975).

[31]Mosteller and Moynihan, *On Equality of Educational Opportunity.*

[32]George Mayeske *et al., A Study of Our Nation's Schools* (Washington, D.C.: Department of Health, Education, and Welfare, 1972).

[33]Smith, in Mosteller and Moynihan, *On Equality of Educational Opportunity.*

[34]D. K. Cohen, T. F. Pettigrew, and R. T. Riley, Race and the outcomes of schooling, in Mosteller and Moynihan, *On Equality of Educational Opportunity.*

[35]Jencks *et al., Inequality.*

[36]*Design for a National Longitudinal Study of School Desegregation* (Santa Monica: Rand Corp., 1974).

[37]Levin, Education, life chances, and the courts.

[38]Robert L. Crain *et al., Southern Schools: An Evaluation of the Effects of the Emergency School Assistance Program* (Chicago: National Opinion Research Center, 1973), vols. 1 and 2.

[39]See, for example, Samuel Bowles, Towards equality of educational opportunity?, 38 *Harvard Educational Review* 89-99 (1968).

[40]Memorandum from George Madaus to Members of the Joint Committee on Test Standards Revision, May 7, 1973; also Frederick Mosher, "Progress Report on the Instrumentation Study," The Huron Institute, June 1974.

[41]Among the earliest critics were Joshua Fishman *et al.,* Guidelines for testing minority children, 20 *Journal of Social Issues* 129-145 (1964).

[42]Crain *et al., Southern Schools.*

[43]Gordon W. Allport, *The Nature of Prejudice* (Garden City: Doubleday Anchor Books, 1954); and Samuel A. Stouffer *et al., The American Soldier* (Princeton: Princeton University Press, 1949).

[44]See St. John, *School Desegregation,* Chapter 4.

[45]James M. Jones, *Prejudice and Racism* (Reading, Mass.: Addison-Wesley, 1972); also St. John, *School Desegregation.*

[46]Judith Porter, *Black Child, White Child* (Cambridge, Mass.: Harvard University Press, 1971).

[47]See, for example, *ibid.,* R. Hope (1967), cited in St. John, *School Desegregation.*

[48]Allan Wicker, Attitudes versus actions: the relationship of verbal and overt behavioral responses to attitude objects, 25 *Journal of Social Issues* 75 (1969).

[49]J. Seidner (1971), described in Elizabeth G. Cohen, The effects of desegregation on race relations, 39 *Law and Contemporary Problems* 271-299 (1975).

[50]I. Katz and L. Benjamin, Effects of white authoritarianism in biracial work groups, 61 *Journal of Abnormal and Social Psychology* 448-456 (1960).

[51]Examples of this kind of research include Crain *et al., Southern Schools;* Appendix C1, U.S.C.C.R., *Racial Isolation;* J. E. Teele and C. Mayo, School racial integration: tumult and shame, 25 *Journal of Social Issues* 137-156 (1969); E. Useem, White students and token desegregation, 10 *Integrated Education* 46-54 (1972); C. Willie and J. Beker, *Race Mixing in the Public Schools* (New York: Praeger, 1973).

[52]Crain *et al., Southern Schools.*

[53]*E.g.*, Cohen, The effects of desegregation, p. 286.

[54]Ray C. Rist, *The Invisible Children: School Integration in American Society* (Cambridge, Mass.: Harvard University Press, forthcoming 1977).

[55]For example, one federal district court judge noted, "much of the current research replies to precise policy based questions with the ambiguity of a Delphic oracle. . . ." *Hart vs.Community School Board*, 383 F. Supp. 699, 744 (E.D.N.Y. 1974).

[56]In *Hobson v. Hansen*, 327 F. Supp. 844, 859 (D.D.C. 1971), Judge J. Skelly Wright commented: "Having hired their respective experts, the lawyers in this case had a basic responsibility, which they have not completely met, to put the hard core statistical demonstrations into language which serious and concerned laymen could, with effort, understand. Moreover, the studies by both experts are tainted by a vice well known in the statistical trade—data shopping and scanning to reach a preconceived result; and the court has had to reject parts of both reports as unreliable because biased. Lest like a latter day version of *Jarndyce vs. Jarndyce* this litigation itself should consume the capital of children in whose behalf it was brought, the court has been forced back to its own common sense approach to a problem which, though admittedly complex, has certainly been made more obscure than was necessary."

[57]Catherine Caldwell shows how the Coleman Report was used this way; see Caldwell, Social science as ammunition, 4 *Psychology Today* 38-41, 72-73 (September 1970).

[58]Some social scientists warn that the federal government's domination of research funding will lead to government domination of research perspectives and of the growth of knowledge. Green urges researchers to deny their services to the existing power structure in order to support countervailing forces whose viewpoints are, he argues, chronically unrepresented. See Philip Green, The obligations of American social scientists, 395 *The Annals of the American Academy of Political and Social Sciences* 13-27 (1971).

[59]Coleman *et al.*, *Trends in School Segregation*.

Courtrooms and Classrooms

Eleanor P. Wolf*

*The freedom the judiciary has from
political responsibility and control makes
its processes more rather than less
appropriate for critical exploration.*[1]

Introduction

It has been reported that when Thurgood Marshall, then acting as counsel in the *Brown* cases, asked historians to search the record for evidence on the intent of the framers of the Fourteenth Amendment with respect to school segregation, the attorney warned that "what looked like a 'golden gate' might turn out to be a booby trap with a bomb in it."[2] When I think of some of the recent accusations of fraud,[3] backlash, beclouding, bias, and collusion,[4] Justice Marshall's statement has a certain prophetic quality.

At present hardly anyone seems pleased with the role of that uncertain ally, the social sciences, in the school segregation cases. Citizens are impatient with experts who appear to say first one thing and then another, and to disagree so much among themselves. Because the general public believes (erroneously) that evidence of the educational or attitudinal benefits of integration are the legal grounds on which these cases are being decided, many are puzzled that courts should impose orders on the basis of such controversial findings. The NAACP is understandably bitter at the

*The research on which this paper is based was made possible by a grant from the Ford Foundation and support from the Center for Urban Studies, Wayne State University.

growing inclination of some former academic allies to be more critical of research claims that in the past were spared close scrutiny and to exercise the obligation of social scientists to change their minds when newer findings do not confirm earlier ones. Although most social scientists have little idea of what is presented to courts in the name of their disciplines, some who have appeared in these cases have serious misgivings about the way in which their findings emerged in the courtroom. In addition, there are those who have struggled, as I have, with the more general problem of an honest and useful role for the social sciences in a great social movement.[5]

Legal scholars appear to be the group most concerned about incompatibilities in the marriage (Alfred Kelly called it an "illicit love affair"[6]) between constitutional principles and empirical research, perhaps because they are both more aware of these .problems—which are, of course, not confined to school segregation cases—and more concerned about the integrity of legal principles. During the years when there were many articles in the law journals about the role played by social science in the 1954 decision, the predominant response from social scientists was one of self-congratulation. Chronically beset by status-anxiety and uncertain self-esteem, the affected disciplines were gladdened by this sign of their importance and respectability: the Supreme Court had taken notice of us, even though only in a footnote.

But Brown was very different from the present school cases. Those not convinced of this should read some of the transcript of that oral argument before the Supreme Court and note the repeated insistence by plaintiff's counsel that their concern is with state-imposed racial exclusion and not with the amount of racial mixture that might or might not come about in various school districts using other modes of assignment. Paul Carrington has described Brown as a "neighborhood school case." The issue presented to the Court was quite unambiguous:

> . . . do not deny any child the right to get to a school of his choice on the grounds of race or color within the normal limits of your districting system . . . do not assign him on a basis of race . . . and we have no complaint. If you have some other basis . . . any other basis, we have no objection. But just do not put in race or color as a factor.[7]

And, responding to the concerns some had expressed about the possible effect of desegregation upon educational standards, NAACP counsel said:

> . . . what we want from this Court is the striking down of race . . . the question is made about the educational level of children . . . they give tests to children—so what do we think is the solution? Simple. Put the dumb colored children in with the dumb white children, and put the smart colored children with the smart white children—that is no problem.[8]

In a recent article, Owen Fiss reports Robert Crain's comment that:

> ... twenty years ago there was no respectable social science evidence tending to show segregation was harmful, and yet social scientists were nearly unanimous in believing that it was. Today there is respectable evidence tending to show that it is harmful but no one in the profession believes it.[9]

This observation is only partly accurate. The appraisal of the *Brown* evidence would hardly be disputed, but Crain's evaluation of recent empirical evidence on the effects of racial concentration is open to some challenge.[10] The reasons for the contrasting attitudes of social scientists, however, are not hard to find. In 1954 the issue was the constitutionality of state laws requiring the separation of the races in school. The support scholars gave to the principle of universal citizenship was hardly different, save perhaps in extent and intensity, from that given by other liberals. Ten years before *Brown*, at the start of World War II, almost one-third of the nation favored desegregated schools. Within two years after *Brown* the proportion had increased to almost half.[11] But the interpretation of *desegregation*, both implicitly and explicitly, rejected any consideration of racial proportions. Recall the headlines: "Nine Pupils *Integrate* Little Rock High School"; "Drive to *Integrate* Lunch Counters." The decision of 1954 seemed to us only simple justice, the long-delayed triumph of the Harlan dissent with its eloquent insistence that "the Constitution is color blind." By contrast, opposition to involuntary dispersion to alter the racial composition of schools ("busing"—because most children who live within walking distance of a city school are of the same race) is very high among whites, divides blacks, has remained quite constant, and has been found to be generally unrelated to many of the usual measures of racial attitudes and beliefs about civil rights.[12]

Brown was not, as some now assert, and only our enemies then alleged, the first step in a campaign designed to end in an attack on racial imbalance, via the courts. It was not until much later, after courts had begun to evaluate the compliance of southern school systems by using the "test of results," that the possibility emerged of adapting this strategy to overcome what used to be called northern *de facto* segregation. The present controversies over the meaning of educational equality did not develop for many years after *Brown*. To the extent that the substandard educational achievement of black children was recognized—and it was *not* widely known nor acknowledged—we assumed that it was entirely caused by inequality of school resources and would disappear with reasonable equalization. We grossly underestimated the strength of the dismal relationship that seems to exist in all countries between academic achievement and social background. "Poor schools" were considered by nearly everyone to be an adequate explanation for poor school work.[13] Comparison of black-white academic achievement within schools was considered an improper and illiberal type of study, and inquiry into the influence of cultural orientations and emphases of various ethnic groups was even more suspect then than it is today. There was some concern about possible injury from *de facto* racial concentration, but most of us expected that the enactment of anti-discrimination legislation and general economic improvement would result in a much greater degree of dispersion than has occurred.

Feagin is only one of many scholars to note that until very recently social researchers did not take into account the factor of ethnic attachment or voluntary congregation "as important in . . . black segregation," although Myrdal had called attention to this determinant decades ago.[14] We also seriously underestimated the indirect effects of black social class distribution in accounting for the residential choices of other groups, and ignored their social ties, as well.

Do the Northern School Cases Need Social Science?

Harm-Benefit Research

Brown needed no help from social science evidence, but some of the northern school cases have made extensive use of such materials. It must be noted that the content of a court ruling may not reveal whether social science evidence on a particular subject was presented during a trial. The *Hobson* opinion of 1967 clearly reflects, as do some others, the influence of testimony on education:

> Racially and socially homogeneous schools damage the minds and spirits of all children. . . . The scholastic achievement of the disadvantaged child, Negro and white, is strongly related to the racial and socio-economic composition of the student body. . . . A racially and socially integrated school environment increases the scholastic achievement of the disadvantaged child of whatever race . . . [later] . . . placing the child in lower tracks for reduced education based on [inappropriate] tests, thus implementing the self-fulfilling prophecy phenomenon inherent in such misjudgments; . . . inferior teachers, textbooks unrelated to the lives of disadvantaged children; inadequate remedial programs . . . all have contributed to the increase in crime, particularly juvenile crime.[15]

By contrast, there was no mention of such evidence in the *Bradley v. Milliken* rulings at either the District Court or Appeals Court level. But during the trial there had been voluminous testimony concerning integration effects on achievement, attitudes, and race relations, research that for brevity's sake I will hereafter refer to as harm-benefit studies, and I think the District Court Judge, Stephen Roth, was deeply influenced by these materials. Present controversy about the validity of harm-benefit studies has reactivated questions about the role of such evidence in judicial proceedings. Perhaps as a consequence of these controversies, the plaintiffs introduced no harm-benefit testimony during the recent trial in Cleveland. Are we moving toward a situation where issues of great concern in these school cases will not be the subject of expert testimony? It was strange enough, after reading the trial record in the Detroit proceedings, to go back to the ruling and see that it was silent on some of the very subjects about which Judge Roth expressed the most intense interest. Perhaps we will now see school cases where what is on everyone's mind is the hidden agenda in the courtroom. Will the views of the judge on harm of segregation, benefit of integration, and thus, ineluctably, the effectiveness of a remedy be formed from his own fragmentary knowledge, snippets of popularized research reported in the press, or whatever materials are brought to his notice by various groups and individuals quite apart from judicial proceedings? (Thus, as Paul Rosen points out, Justice Holmes' opinion upholding a compulsory sterilization law reflected popular versions of Spencer and misinterpretations of Darwin, although Holmes had never read either: it was simply "in the air."[17]) And will this also mean that we are now bound by legal precedents that were established in previous cases where decisions were influenced by evidence now widely conceded to have been seriously inadequate or defective? Much of the widely ranging testimony on education in *Bradley v. Milliken*, for example, was of poor quality. But the agreement of experts on both sides concerning the alleged benefits to both academic achievement and race relations that would be forthcoming from racially-mixed schools was clearly influential in causing Judge Roth to alter his pre-trial opposition to involuntary student re-assignment for integration.[18]

The "De Facto-is-Really-De Jure" Alternative

The present inconclusive nature of harm-benefit research findings has perhaps contributed to the shift in emphasis in northern school segregation cases. In the effort to assimilate them to *Brown*, evidence is required to show that *de facto* is really *de jure*. If predominantly black schools in Detroit are, like those in pre-1954 Mississippi, the product of government's segregatory practices, both systems are unconstitutional and for the same reason. The only necessity is to show that it was state action that produced the patterns of racial imbalance in Northern schools. To demonstrate this, two lines of causal analysis have been used: constitutional violations by school authorities and/or state actions that aided descrimination in housing and are thus responsible indirectly for the condition of racial separation in schools.

School Violations Approach

Since the Supreme Court has not yet ruled that geographical assignment of students who live in racially segregated neighborhoods is a constitutional violation, the key approach in the recent school cases is to show that school system "cheating"—various forms of segregatory practices or racial discrimination, often in the past—was an important cause of the racial concentration that now exists. Fiss has characterized the "theory" as one contrived to maintain continuity with *Brown*.[19] Although plaintiffs sometimes describe these cases as "straight-out violations of the Fourteenth Amendment," a trial that requires, as it did in Detroit, a good portion of 42 days to establish this is perhaps not so very straight-out after all. The evidence presented involved an enormous amount of demographic materials and school records of various kinds: maps, charts, historical documents, citizens' reports, as well as oral testimony on school policies and practices over a period of about twenty years. In the attempt to show system-wide effects of specific violations, there was a considerable use of concepts from the social sciences such as "perception of segregation," "feelings of containment," "debilitation of school image," as well as some unsupported claims of reciprocal effects on housing segregation, including the contention that some of these practices contributed to residential instability or "white flight."

I know of no competent sociologist in this field who considers racial imbalance in northern urban schools to be in any substantial way anything other than the reflection of residential patterns. Findings of constitutional violations enable a judge, who is sincerely convinced by what he has heard (in or out of court) that the condition of racial concentration is harmful, to use judicial power to reassign students and thus to correct this condition. It is the most dependable legal "trigger" available to "fire the cannon" of school desegregation, to use Owen Fiss' language.[20]

If specific acts of racial discrimination (within the still-permissible system of assignment to the school nearest a child's home) were to be taken seriously as a cause of system-wide racial separation in northern schools, a rather elaborate kind of demographic and sociological analysis would have to be developed. In the Detroit trial, not only was the evidence (in my view, but not in that of the Appeals Court!) quite inadequate, but the parallel body of testimony on residential segregation was, as I will show later, inconsistent with a theory that the racial imbalance in the schools was caused by school system violations. Given the fact that so many northern schools that are now predominantly black were once white, some kind of sociological analysis would be needed to demonstrate that this process—one that affected all other residentially-based agencies and institutions just as it did schools—would have been in some way different if school authorities had not committed their unconstitutional actions. Generally, such causal analysis is based on implicit or poorly specified hypotheses about the effects of school system actions on the residential decisions of black and white households, but *unlawful acts* (a legal concept) are not necessarily *causes* (a scientific concept) of a societal condition. If the school violations approach becomes the sole basis for desegregation orders, perhaps courts will expect better evidence of this doctrine than was offered in Detroit, especially as judges become more aware of the ambiguous findings of harm-benefit research. But if the burden of proof is shifted to school authorities, who must prove that nothing they (ever?) did contributed to racial concentration, no such analysis will be required, for this formulation converts a vague theory of highly doubtful validity into a proposition that seems untestable. (At least I cannot conceive of a research design to investigate it, but others may be more ingenious.)

There is another consequence of this approach that requires some consideration. The ruling that Detroit school officials, black and white, who had been widely regarded as strongly pro-integration, had been engaged in deliberate racial segregation cannot avoid a strong accusatory element. No one has yet studied the effects, if any, upon the public of the use of this strategy. At public meetings of Regional School Boards in Detroit, I have observed responses of confusion, bewilderment, cynicism (much in line with current appraisals of government, perhaps), and the suspicion that the courts are using legal tricks. But as I noted earlier, the general belief of most people (who do not go to meetings of any kind) seems to be that the court decisions result from judges' conviction that "racial balance" is good for education. At present, however, in Detroit, where the proportion of white students is about 25%, this explanation, too, is a source of confusion.

State Complicity in Housing Discrimination

The second type of causal analysis involves the use of social science testimony to show the extent and degree of racial separation in urban neighborhoods and identifies racial discrimination against blacks, aided and abetted by government, as its chief cause. Demographic and sociological testimony, with some use of social psychological concepts as well, comes to the forefront, rather than the educational-attitudinal effects of various school factors. This housing discrimination approach seems the most likely basis on which to compel the inclusion of suburban communities in court-ordered busing programs, for they, too, to judge from the Supreme Court's ruling on Detroit, require a prior finding of *de jure* segregation before busing orders can be imposed—and even the most gifted legal team will find it difficult to prove school-system violations against black children in communities where there are none. Although the legal use of the residential patterns and housing materials was rejected by the Appeals Court, this testimony, like that on education, had a powerful effect on Judge Roth. His sense of injustice was deeply affected by the shameful record of discrimination in housing, and the great emphasis he placed on residential segregation in his ruling accorded nicely with his obvious reluctance to "blame" a school system that had had a strongly pro-integration leadership for the past several years.[21] It also convinced him that the only path to any substantial degree of racial/class mixture in the Detroit area in the foreseeable future was to divorce school assignment from place of residence. But the narrow perspective of the housing testimony ignored the indirect effects of own-group preferences of other ethnic groups and minimized those of blacks, and stressed white exclusion and *"flight"* while neglecting *avoidance* and the "realistic" factors that contribute to it, causing him to seriously underestimate the difficulties inherent in the remedy to which he was attracted.

A Non-Empirical Alternative?

Mark Yudof's admirably expressed criticisms of both harm-benefit analysis and the constitutional violations approach as grounds for court-ordered racial dispersion lead him to consider the possibility of the universalist ethic as an alternative.[22] It is not clear to me whether he considers it constitutionally adequate ("it may not serve"), and, if so, on what grounds. The open declaration of assimilation ("a shared culture") as a goal for public education would have the merit of candor, for the conception of society underlying some of these decisions is indeed of this nature. In the final section of Judge Roth's ruling in Detroit, for example, all ethnic concentrations, past and present, voluntary or not, are cast in negative terms.[23]

But on what basis does the judiciary impose its vision of the good society upon others? Legislative and administrative-policy provisions to compel or persuade school systems to correct imbalanced schools have used language reflecting some version of a universalist ethic, but these measures require some degree of public support for enactment, to say nothing of compliance. The need for empirical verification is not avoided either, because the case for mandatory integration is argued largely in instrumental terms: An integrated society is required, a racially separated one rejected, in terms of their effects:

> . . . a stable just society without violence, alienation and social discord must be an integrated society. Segregation of the races in public institutions, employment and housing will inevitably lead to conflict and the destruction of democratic values and institutions.[24]

Segregation cannot here mean discrimination or racial exclusion, for these have long since been outlawed. The reference must be to a condition of racial concentration without regard to cause; integration as Yudof uses it here must mean dispersion, not open access. The contention, then, is that the involuntary redistribution of students to achieve racially mixed schools is a societal necessity. It is asserted that racial concentration leads to conflict and the eventual destruction of democratic society; dispersion is a necessary although, no doubt, an insufficient condition in order to avoid violence, alienation, and social discord. These are all empirical propositions, versions of the contact hypothesis in race relations, albeit on a considerably larger scale than those we are usually called upon to deal with. Further, the case for the school as the most effective arena for the work of societal unification rests upon empirical propositions related both to efficacy (e.g., schools reach people at an early age) and to various feasibility considerations of cost, control, and scope.

None of these propositions is self-evident; and there is enough contrary evidence from both this and other societies to justify a considerable degree of skepticism.[25] Stability and the absence of social discord do not necessarily co-exist with "justice," and there are other social reforms that offer more promise of creating a just society than does involuntary racial dispersion. Conflict avoidance is a goal with doubtful ethical claims, as well as empirical uncertainty, in a multi-group society. My point here is that once again "social science" has not been avoided; only the subject matter has changed. Instead of emphasis on peer effects on academic achievement, we have shifted to larger and more difficult areas, but not avoiding empirical challenges to contact effects in the classroom. Merely by way of suggesting the complexity of the issues involved, we may recall that the nation responsible for the murder of several million Jews and other members of "inferior races" had one of the highest Jewish-non-Jewish intermarriage rates in the pre-World War II world. Decreasing social distance and abundant interpersonal contact may have as little to do with preventing the erosion of democratic institutions as getting-to-know-our-friends-from-abroad has to do with avoiding wars.

Can Social Science be Removed from the Remedy?

It might be possible to reduce the use of social science in these school cases by excluding from consideration all subjects except school system practices. But how can the courts avoid harm-benefit issues when fashioning a remedy, whatever the basis on which the ruling is made, including attempts to "de-empiricalize" it, as Yudof has suggested?

I see only two alternatives, neither of which has prevailed. The first would be to give up the attempt to unravel history and simply order the school authorities to cease their violations. But since most of these were committed in the past and, in my opinion, had little to do with the creation of racially imbalanced schools anyhow, this would probably have no noticeable effects, if effects are to be measured in terms of racial composition. The other alternative is to define the desegregation remedy as a permanent system of racial quota assignments within the confines of whatever district has been found guilty of *de jure* segregation, without regard for its proportion of blacks. If this definition is adopted, no social science is required and a desegregation plan can be produced by computer and transportation technicians.

This definition, which NAACP describes as the creation of "racially unidentifiable schools" (with allowances for certain practicalities and with little if anything said about future re-assignments to maintain uniform racial proportions), is close to the position described by their desegregation expert during the Detroit-only remedy hearings in 1972, who offered, when challenged, a number of unsupported assertions about the educational and psychological benefits to be derived from attendance at schools of roughly uniform racial composition, irrespective of the proportion of blacks.[26] If this approach to a desegregation remedy is rejected, however, there is no way to avoid the numerous cost-benefit calculations that may have been kept underground during the trial and it is during this process that social science must collide with law.[27] We may liken it to the futile efforts to combine social science with law in the sentencing of a prisoner. There is always the danger, when the judge asks for expert guidance as to what type of prison and for what length of time would be best to maximize the chances of rehabilitation, that he will be told that there is really no evidence that any such measures are rehabilitative. At this point, the judge must either alter his purpose or shop for some other experts. At the remedy stage in these school cases, the basic decision about the size of the area, and thus its racial and social class proportions, has already been determined by the legal doctrine that the "nature of the remedy is determined by the scope of the violation."[28] Thus all the endless discussions during the metropolitan hearings conducted by Judge Roth concerning how far the desegregation area should extend in order to secure optimum racial and social class proportions were for nothing. The decision was made by the Supreme Court on a legal basis: Detroit, but not its suburbs, had been found guilty of segregation *de jure.*

During the 1972 remedy hearings in Detroit, as in some other cases, the judge seemed to be trying to fashion a plan that would maximize mixture, while preserving other educational goals, and offer the greatest promise of maintaining residential stability. Serious consideration of these objectives by experts best qualified to do so runs the risk of raising questions that had not been critically examined, perhaps not even mentioned, during the trial. There is a whole series of assumptions concerning the potency of schooling, the relationship between attitudes and overt behavior, the factors in residential decision-making, the effects of interracial contact, and the relationship between academic achievement and other variables that, if they became the subject of first-rate testimony reflecting varied perspectives at this point, would throw these proceedings into confusion. Yet unless the mechanical approach to desegregation is adopted, or the "cease discrimination" command substituted, some kind of social science *will* be involved in remedy proceedings, although its role is unclear and uncertain.

Serious cost-benefit discussions cannot avoid the introduction of social science evidence that constantly trespasses on forbidden territory (as will be shown later), although by the time the remedy stage is reached, some sort of legal Rubicon has been crossed. I leave it to the legal experts to explain what would happen if it were discovered that there was *no* achievable plan that could provide *any* discernible benefit. Fortunately, our disciplines are not likely to produce anything so definite.

The Two Worlds of Law and Social Science

If my judgment is correct that there is no reasonable way to exclude the consideration of social science materials completely from these school cases at either the trial or remedy stage, what are the most serious problems the use of this material encounters in the courtroom? To what extent do these difficulties reflect a fundamental incompatibility between the two worlds of science and the law; to what extent might they be overcome by procedural improvements?

The Education of a Judge

When I first began to read the trial record of *Bradley v. Milliken* and saw the elaborate statistical presentations, the heavy use of terms from quantitative research, and the numerous arguments about the propriety of using various techniques of data analysis, it seemed altogether unreasonable to expect any layman to follow the testimony. Judge Wright refers to this kind of problem when he observed:

> The unfortunate if inevitable tendency has been to lose sight of the disadvantaged young students . . . in an over-grown garden of numbers and charts and jargon like "standard deviation of the variable" . . . "statistical significance" and "Pearson product moment correlations." . . .[29]

But later I decided that this kind of problem need be only a minor obstacle to a judge's understanding. Certainly with respect to the materials offered in the Detroit case, the analytical techniques most appropriate, given the crudeness and inadequacies of the available data, were well within the capacity of experts to explain and judges to comprehend. The distinction between the meaning of the term "significant," as used in common speech and in non-sampling procedures, and its meaning in sample statistics was well explained and understood with little difficulty. The truly unfortunate aspect of much of the statistical materials presented was that they created an impression of rigor and precision that was misleading. I suspect their purpose was to impress the judge.[30]

It is not difficult to explain to an intelligent layman, in plain English, that unless we have information on entry-level differences in academic proficiency, we cannot arrive at conclusions about the effects of school inputs, but this was never done, although there were elaborate statistical presentations of these inputs, right down to school site acreage! (But it appeared later that the distinction between the term *input* and socioeconomic status had not been made clear to the judge; I suspect everyone thought someone else had done it.) Nor is it impossible to alert a judge to the need to distinguish between the effects of socioeconomic status of the child and SES effects of his peers, a distinction often blurred in experts' testimony. It was not the formidable statistical demonstrations that were responsible for an array of inaccurate information given by expert witnesses to the judge: e.g., that "black parents have never opposed busing as a concept," or that "the black-white achievement gap . . . closes in mixed schools," or that the standard error of the mean "corrects for cultural bias in testing," or that school-wide averages in mixed schools tell us that black children in those schools are doing better, etc., etc. Adversary procedures encourage the use of strongly partisan experts (especially if it is calculated that their personal characteristics will favorably influence the judge) while discouraging the participation of others who may be better qualified. But this is only one of the factors that obstructs the process of "informing the judicial mind." Virtually every feature of the courtroom hinders the learning process. The principle that guides everything that takes place within it is winning the case, whether this aim is fervidly or half-heartedly pursued. Legal advantage determines what will be presented, and when (if possible) and how, and by whom. The calculation of legal advantage determines whether an error will be corrected and a misunderstanding clarified—or simply added to the steadily mounting accumulation of confusions and contradictions.

In *Milliken*, the student-judge was clearly intelligent, industrious, and deeply interested in most of the subject matter. It was he, and only he, who (during the sessions on residential patterns) raised the question of whether black Americans "are a cultural group," saying: "I have the impression they think they are." He asked a number of questions about the clustering of white ethnic groups, although it did not occur to him that this would have important consequences for the spatial isolation of blacks, and no one pointed this out. He persistently sought to learn whether community control and extensive student dispersion could co-exist. He was so skeptical about the assertions of plaintiff's education expert that there was little difference between the school entry-level proficiency of black and white children that he interrupted this testimony to ask a number of questions. He tried to find out whether experts think school size is important and whether instability in school assignment is disadvantageous. He tried to ascertain the consensus of scholarly opinion on whether early deprivation can be overcome by compensatory education, and if there was an age after which unfavorable effects were irreversible. He twice asked about birthrate differentials, during a presentation on projected racial proportions of the student population.

Most of these questions and many others he asked were answered poorly or not at all. But my point here is to illustrate the kinds of inquiries raised in cases of this kind. They have nothing to do with specific events and individuals. These are much like the questions raised by a bright student in a seminar on "Education and Urban Society." Even for the purpose of ordinary fact-finding, adversary procedures have been severely criticized. In one well-known discussion of this matter, for example, Jerome Frank considers the defects of the "fight-theory," pointing out that it encourages errors and omissions as a result of the deliberate use of stress, intimidation, and cunning to discredit adverse witnesses and to conceal information that is helpful to opposing parties, concluding with the famous line: "Our present trial method is thus the equivalent of throwing pepper in the eyes of a surgeon when he is performing an operation."[31] As a method for responding adequately to the kinds of inquiries raised by Judge Roth in the Detroit proceedings, the setting and procedures of the courtroom are grotesquely inappropriate.

From beginning to end, this strange "seminar" is organized and conducted in a manner that defeats educational aims at every turn. The student comes without having taken any of the prerequisite courses, so that he is unacquainted with both the subject matter and the basic logic of scientific inquiry. He appears to be trying to do his homework in class, as well he might, for the trial is lengthy and exhausting. He has no list of required readings and no one with whom he can hash over the content of what is said each day. He is presented with a hodgepodge of topics from an educational point of view. First the plaintiffs offer highly selective testimony, the content of which is determined by counsel in accord with their calculations of what is strategically advantageous. Days—or weeks—go by, and eventually defendant's experts return to these same subjects. Those who give the testimony for each side, on the same topic, do not interact so that they can resolve differences that are reducible to facts, or clearly expose and elucidate those that arise from differing evaluations. Their interaction takes place in a strangely circuitous manner, via intermediaries. Whatever systematic presentation of issues is possible within this framework is further hampered by unavoidable problems of when various witnesses (or even counsel specializing in certain subjects) can be on hand.

There is no one in the courtroom who has a teaching role, that is, there is no person whose sole function is to clarify, elucidate, reveal misunderstandings, sort out confusions, and make sure that key terms are defined, understood, and used consistently, at least by the same speaker. The impediments to learning appear to be inherent in adversary procedures and are reflected in courtroom etiquette. To illustrate: the judge, thinking back, one guesses, to his own pre-trial statement, in which he had spoken so critically of involuntary student re-assignment to promote racial balance, asked an expert witness: "Can you achieve integration of the schools in this city, or any other city, simply by the numbers?"[32] If such a question were asked in class, a teacher would respond by saying something like: I cannot answer that until you explain what you have in mind when you use the term *integration*. Then, at appropriate points in the ensuing dialogue, one would ask: Does your phrase *simply by the numbers* imply that you define integration as some level of biracial social *interaction*, rather than the presence of certain proportions (what proportions?) of black and white students? Are you thinking of some effects on educational achievement? Race relations? If you consider certain proportions of blacks and whites a necessary, although not a sufficient, condition to secure the kind of *integration* you have in mind, are you concerned in your question with how to *maintain* that mixture?

Such inquiries were not forthcoming. It was perhaps not serious that no party was willing to correct the judge's obvious confusion between the meaning of *variation* and *variable*.[33] But it was important that the contradiction be explored between testimony that severe disadvantage in social background tends to hamper intellectual development and testimony that educational failure in large part occurs because teachers in poor black schools "don't perceive that those children learn just as readily as children from high-income families."[34] There was no one whose legal advantage was served by saying: Judge, please take note. You have a serious contradiction here that must be examined. Does poverty or some associated background disadvantage really have an adverse effect, or do some teachers *mistakenly* believe that it does, and it is their false belief that causes the poor performance?

After a presentation on educational resource allocations, the judge referred the next day to that testimony as assuming that teacher competence depends on seniority—although the expert had twice pointed out that he made no such assumption. But the man was gone, never to return, and it was not in the interests of either side to correct this misinterpretation. It suited the NAACP to let stand the statement that teachers of lower seniority were of lesser competence because it strengthened their contention of some discrimination in resource allocation to predominantly black schools. The defendant school board was not eager to emphasize that its salary schedule had a doubtful empirical basis. So nobody said anything, whereupon the error was compounded by the judge's asking the expert witness then before him whether it might not instead be true that "after a certain level of competence . . . additional years . . . might diminish ability?" Instead of reminding the court of earlier testimony that the effects of teacher characteristics on learning are far from clear, the expert opined it probably depended on the individual, a reply that encouraged the judge to jettison all social science generalizations: ". . . they are all individuals, aren't they . . . isn't that one of the difficulties?"[35] Here was an opportunity to explain that all social science knowledge consists of generalizations, with varying degrees of verification, that we operate on the assumption that it is possible to develop them despite individual differences, etc. But nothing was said except to indicate agreement.

In fact, there was a large amount of agreeing with the judge, fulsome flattery, in addition to the expected deference. Sometimes people praised him for saying something when in fact he had said the opposite. For a student to have such power over his teachers is not helpful to learning, but it is hard to see how this problem can be appreciably lessened within adversary proceedings.

Getting the Facts

To a social researcher, the use of adversary procedures to secure accurate data about factual matters such as educational resource allocations, or whether school "A" did or did not have space in the winter term of 1969 for 240 children, is absurd. It is like staging a public debate on the subject: What is the population of Washington, D.C.? There are not two sides to purely factual matters of this kind any more than there are two answers to a problem in arithmetic, nor is the answer somewhere in the middle. Since carefully reviewing some portions of the school violations testimony in the Detroit case in great detail and checking validity as one would in any research project, I have concluded that ascertaining facts by listening to competing oral testimony on this topic worked rather poorly. Some of the material was incorrect, some was of doubtful accuracy, and some was so internally inconsistent that it is difficult to understand how the court came to certain conclusions.

Equally dubious as a method of obtaining accurate and complete information on explosive themes is to seek it from public school officials who are asked to testify in public in a tense and troubled city. In such a situation, a researcher would use a skilled and sensitive interviewer who could assure his subject complete anonymity and absolute confidentiality of the material. There is a long list of topics that no school official in his right mind would discuss fully and frankly in an open courtroom; he has to maintain rapport with various groups within the city, regardless of the trial's outcome. People in such positions rarely say anything in public that might be offensive to any ethnic group, are afraid to admit that somewhere there is a child who is not very bright, or that there is serious delinquency and crime in and near some city schools (without quickly balancing this with a reference to sin in suburbia). They must always express positive and encouraging evaluations, lest they be accused of low expectations, and are given to various cliches and platitudes that serve to protect those who are in delicate and vulnerable positions. In general, their testimony consistently attributes to schools and schooling a capacity and power to alter both individuals and society far beyond what has been demonstrated or is even reasonable in terms of existing theory.

The Content of Social Science Testimony

Adversary proceedings cannot be depended upon to ensure the emergence of important bodies of testimony involved in social policy questions nor to ensure that the aspects of these topics that are of greatest significance will be seen as relevant by the litigants—or by the judge. They use different standards. Calculations of various kinds of legal advantage determined to a great extent what social science testimony would be presented in Detroit.

From a study of the record, it appears that Judge Roth's chief concerns throughout the trial were shaped by the question of the desegregation remedy: Would it be effective? Was it feasible? The testimony on education spoke to the first of these concerns. The testimony on residential patterns had the *effect* of obscuring the issues involved in the question of feasibility.

As early as the fourth day of the trial, the Judge raised the question about the probable consequences on residential movement of a busing order. Would it lead to "abandonment by . . . white folks so . . . you'd have a city no more integrated than when you started . . . ?"[36] An adequate answer, i.e., a presentation of what is known and not known about residential decision-making, was never forthcoming. Testimony on housing and residential movements was presented only by plaintiffs, to support their legal position and to reveal the extent to which government had supported or permitted violations of the rights of black citizens. Testimony on exclusionary practices and incidents of intimidation was impressive. But the general import of the entire body of housing material was that residential patterns were overwhelmingly the result of discrimination caused by prejudice (by definition an irrational response) for which, at least by implication, interracial contact would be a helpful antidote. Even the explanation of how the segregation index is calculated, which began with the warning that it merely measures departure from a random distribution with no reference to causation, was soon ignored and the index was equated with racial discrimination: Within the week, Judge Roth, requesting a summary of segregation trends, asked: "Are the forces of good overcoming the forces of evil? That's what it comes down to as far as housing segregation is concerned."[37]

Defendants offered no testimony on residential patterns, in accord with their legal position that the issue was not relevant to the charge of constitutional violations within the school system. In any case, the presentation of competing perspectives on such a topic does not fit into an adversary framework. There is no "pro and con" on residential behavior; it is a many-faceted phenomenon involving a complex range of issues. The consequence of this legal determination of the content of testimony was to present the judge with an oversimplified and misleading picture of how black and white residential decisions are made, a description that omitted many crucial components. One that has special relevance was the absence of testimony on the causes of racial transition. Thousands of northern schools at some point in time approximated the condition courts now seek to create. What happened to them? And what conditions are required to keep this from happening in the future, whether students are mixed as a consequence of court orders or of residential change? What is the probable effect of the absence of economic sifting, i.e., a greater degree of social class heterogeneity than usually exists in transition areas? (Why were mixed schools so ineffective from an educational point of view?) The consideration of these and many other relevant questions had no legal advantage for either party; therefore, testimony on them never emerged.

I have said that, despite its absence from the rulings of both district and appeals courts, there was voluminous testimony on education that I judged to be a decisive influence in this case. Here the testimony was gravely defective, in large part, perhaps, because the adversaries were in essential agreement as to the strongly beneficial effects of classroom heterogeneity on academic achievement, race relations, self-conceptions, and aspirations, as well as on equalization of educational resources. If one were to read the whole of this testimony and compare it with, for example, the synthesis of research and theory presented in Nancy St. John's book,[38] one would hardly believe that they dealt with the same subject. The materials presented to the court conveyed an inaccurate description of social science findings and seriously exaggerated the extent to which alleged benefits are forthcoming, but unanimity of opinion appeared to have a powerful effect.

Would a strongly adversarial school board have challenged this misleading testimony and thus revealed its inadequacies? Even if the court permitted it (a doubtful assumption that I will consider later), such a response is by no means assured. It seems quite possible that a school system accused of segregatory practices might well decide that testimony to question the benefits of racial dispersion was a risky legal strategy. If, as Fiss says,[39] school authorities may now be virtually in the position of having to prove that they did not contribute to racial concentration, they might calculate that such material would cast doubt on their innocence. Even the Detroit area suburbs, which did not enter the proceedings until the remedy stage, might have deemed it unwise to challenge harm-benefit assertions if they had been defendants accused of constitutional violations. Adversary proceedings, whether feeble or vigorous, cannot be relied on to provide adequate social science testimony. Nor is it likely that presentations of what is known about harm-benefit effects could be fitted into the pro-con adversary framework in a way that simultaneously meets the needs of litigants and encourages the participation of those best qualified by the standards of social science.

Judicial proceedings cannot be relied on either to reveal or to resolve important discrepancies or contradictions within the context of the social science testimony that is presented. For example, social class differences were heavily relied on to explain the substandard achievement of the city's black children, but the testimony on residential behavior had consistently minimized these differences. Within social science, such a disjunction must be resolved or reconciled. Where were all these poor black families—and their children—during the housing testimony? If their proportion is so great and the influence of disadvantage has so powerful an impact on behavior, will this not affect the residential decisions of whites and thus be an important contributor to spatial separation from blacks? What are the implications of this social class distribution for the expectations that contact between black and white students will "correct stereotypes," a claim constantly reiterated? What does this mean for future stability of any remedy? The procedures of scientific inquiry and presentation would compel attention to these and other unresolved discrepancies that, in the courtroom, can be left hanging in mid-air because it served the advantage of neither side to explore them.

Fundamental Conflicts

The problem of ensuring that better and more inclusive testimony will come before the court might be handled by removing such materials entirely (along with the massive fact-finding tasks discussed earlier) from adversary proceedings. They would be submitted to judges through other mechanisms that, among other advantages, would be far more to the liking of most social scientists.[40] But some basic conflicts between the worlds of law and science that appear to be related to the exercise of judicial authority would remain.[41]

For example, in the Detroit trial two alternative causal analyses were presented that had the effect of explaining the same result without any attempt to integrate or reconcile them, or to offer them as alternative explanations for which evidence adequate to select one rather than the other is as yet lacking. Testimony was offered as follows: (1) The city's neighborhoods are shown to be almost entirely separated by race, and (2) residential location is not directly challenged as a permissible mode of student assignment, but (3) racial separation in the school system is simultaneously said to be caused to a substantial degree by school system cheating, or violations of a geographical assignment system, *which, if followed scrupulously, would have to result in a degree of separation at least as great as what already exists.* The only attempt to reconcile these alternative explanations was a feeble effort to link them by the use of judicial authority: the reiteration of the use in previous school cases of a theory of "corresponding effect," with no presentation of empirical evidence that might resolve this logical inconsistency. I conjecture that this mode of simultaneous presentation appears reasonable in law because the litigants are appealing to a *judge,* offering him two possibilities from which he may make a choice, rather than presenting material that claims to be part of a coherent and consistent body of knowledge.

The content of the decision rendered by the Sixth Circuit Court of

Appeals shows why the offer of these alternative lines of causal analysis by plaintiffs suits the needs of judicial proceedings, no matter how much it violates the canons of scientific explanation: that court rejected the residential segregation approach not because the members evaluated it as false, i.e., lacking empirical support, but because (as I understand it) it was too great a departure from a viewpoint of legal precedent, a consideration wholly irrelevant to science.

Science cannot operate within a framework of pre-determined conclusions, whether these operate by elevating earlier findings to dogma or by substituting judicial authority for scientific verification. The transition from *Brown* to the northern school cases was made with much help from social science material on harm-benefit research. But in law these decisions then appear to acquire the power of precedent despite the inadequacy or inaccuracy of much of the evidence that was an important element in causing them to have been decided as they were. It adds not one iota of support to a scientific generalization to relate how many judges have mentioned it in court decisions; this is simply irrelevant. The problem of incorporating the revision of scientific knowledge into the framework of law was illustrated by Judge Roth's apparent uneasiness about new research that had appeared after his ruling of September 1971. He asked an expert witness at the start of remedy hearings if the newly-published volume "by Mosteller and Moynihan in any way shakes the general conclusions reached by the so-called Coleman Commission," which had been so frequently, and often inaccurately, quoted during the trial, and was told only that although the studies "claimed to reaffirm the Coleman data on the insignificant impact of school resource variation" upon achievement variation, the reanalyses, like the Report, were still in error.[42] He was also told that the "Coleman Report's holding that racial composition of the classroom had a strong effect on achievement had been found erroneous . . . it is a social class, not a racial effect."[43] (Nothing was said of the materials that indicated peer effects were somewhat more doubtful than had previously appeared to be the case.) The judge later permitted suburban counsel's cross-examination on a just-published article by Coleman[44] warning courts about the peril of basing remedies on exaggerated estimates of peer-group effects, but both counsel and expert completely failed to convey the substance of the article.[45]

It is hard to see how the legal framework could have accommodated a solid refutation of exaggerated harm-benefit research if such evidence had been presented in response to a judge's inquiry. NAACP had objected to the introduction of the Coleman article, not because the ruling of segregation had already been made, but as "an attempt to argue for separate but equal." The judge agreed, but said he would "hear it anyway."[46] There was voluminous "social science" testimony throughout these hearings on the extent to which including more whites (by increasing the size of the area) made a "sufficient contribution" to the effectiveness of the classroom mix—or to the diminished danger of "white flight"—to "justify" the length of the journey and other costs. But when suburban counsels' questions edged over into forbidden territory ("How do you know it makes a contribution?"), the inquiry was halted. Although the judge had announced before the hearings began that the "goal was quality education for all children," there were strict but somewhat unclear limits as to what this included. Should kindergarten children be bused? Testimony was offered to support contentions about early learning and the development of racial attitudes. Were the predicted benefits large enough to justify one and one-half hours of travel time for a kindergartener's three-hour day? Expert witnesses (suburbs had none) agreed that they were. When suburban counsel demanded evidence for such assessments, NAACP objected and the court generally upheld them, e.g.,

> . . . you insist on re-opening a question passed long ago . . . you are arguing
> the point that desegregation will result in quality education. . . . That is a
> matter no longer open to question in this case. What we are about is what
> metropolitan plan will do the job.[47]

From a social science perspective, this is illogical. Suppose no metropolitan plan will do the job? (What job?) Or suppose it (desegregation? defined how?) will make so small a contribution to the "job" that it (what, exactly?) does not seem worthwhile? Here the NAACP position (as I understand it) is more logical: A finding of *de jure* segregation compels the creation of "racially unidentifiable" schools, operationally defined as of approximately uniform racial composition. We assert that this is beneficial and we do not have to prove it. Even if you offered empirical evidence that these schools depressed achievement and conferred no other benefits, they are still required. But we will avoid this embarrassment by invoking legal barriers to the production of contrary evidence.[48]

Judge Roth had said that the time for questions concerning benefits had been passed *long ago*. How long ago? I.e., would the court have allowed evidence to challenge the positive effects of school racial mixture if there had been anyone during the trial to offer it? Yudof says:

> With rare exceptions courts have not allowed school boards or white
> intervenors to introduce social science data and testimony to contradict the
> *Brown* result.[49]

This question was answered in Detroit when the court ruled that David Armor's testimony[50] reporting some inconclusive and some negative findings from a number of desegregation studies was inadmissible. Judge Roth first stated that, following upon a finding of segregation *de jure*, "any education theory having the effect of maintaining a pattern of *de jure* segregation is impermissible." A court ruling cannot make a scientific theory impermissible, whether it be the germ theory of disease or any other. Perhaps the wording was unfortunate and he meant only that this material was no longer relevant, since a ruling of segregation *de jure* had already been made in this case? The final paragraph of the ruling, however, suggests otherwise:

> In any event, the Court of Appeals for the Sixth Circuit held on June 10, 1970 that greater, not less desegregation is the proper manner to alleviate the problem of disparity in achievement.[51]

Why then was all that testimony of role models, teachers' expectations, self-images, aspirations, reading scores, social class vs. race effects, testing and tracking, and the rest presented during the 1971 trial? What possible contribution could any study of acheivement make after June 10, 1970? "The Sixth Circuit held . . . ." I see Galileo being led away and hear his insistent voice murmuring, according to legend: "And yet—it moves."

Some Implications

The Detroit decision was upheld on the basis of violations by school authorities, but social science evidence was an essential ingredient in persuading the District Court that racially concentrated schools were harmful and built on an unjust foundation of racial discrimination in housing, that mixed schools were in all ways beneficial, and that these benefits could be achieved through court action. Evidence to cast doubt on the benefits of mixture would perhaps not have been permitted. Systematic consideration of remedy feasibility, i.e., consequences, is not relevant prior to a ruling of segregation *de jure*, but at the remedy stage the court is in the position of seeking guidance in implementing a decision that has already been made. Experts then are asked to weigh benefits vs. costs, but may not consider whether there are, in fact, any benefits. The feasibility of a desegregation remedy involves, among other factors, an estimation of future residential behavior. (Ironically, such a consideration may be defined as a constitutional violation if it restrains the integration efforts of a school board.) But the area to be desegregated has already been determined by court decision, and if experts were to testify that the most likely consequence of a busing order was the acceleration of racial change, judicial response to this prediction would appear to be limited to making the order as modest as is legally permissible. Thus the involvement of "social science" at the remedy stage is either somewhat spurious, or is limited to technical expertise, administrative wisdom, or the development of community sentiment and the formulation of various rationalizations to support the remedy mandated by the courts. In Detroit at present, the most compelling of these has been the need to obey the law.

Drastic changes in the presentation of social science materials that would virtually remove such testimony from adversary proceedings would be required to overcome most of the problems discussed in this paper. This would mean an altogether different role for social science in judicial decision-making in these cases. The fundamental conflict between science and judicial authority is not thereby resolved, but this is one case where, if you are unequal, it is better to be separate.

What would have happened, in the Detroit case, if Judge Roth had been presented with a more complete range of first-class social science materials on the nature of the problems involved and the effectiveness of the remedy within the power of the courts to command? I think it quite likely that there would have been a different ruling. Whether this outcome would make you more or less unhappy depends on your appraisals from social science knowledge, value priorities, and estimates of alternative strategies to achieve more equality in both schools and society. My own conclusion is that, when there is so large a component of doubt concerning the adequacy of constitutional grounds,[52] the benefits of involuntary dispersion, and the feasibility of the busing remedy, it is better for a court to limit its power of compulsion to requiring an end to whatever racial discrimination was found to exist and to providing the dispersion alternative to those black students who wish it.

If government actions were really the chief cause, directly or indirectly, of racially-concentrated schools, or if public opposition to busing were based entirely on irrational fears, racism, and unrealistic estimates of self-interest, the remedy would have a substantial assurance of success built into it. But the program appeals neither to self-interest in any immediate sense nor to the sense of justice that was in some measure available as a source of support, albeit often grudging, for *Brown* and its more easily recognized progeny.

The boldness of the courts in this field of social policy is made possible by their ability to act without public consent, but for outcomes that require the participation of hundreds of thousands of people this freedom is an illusion. I do not refer to the problems of violence or overt protest; these are poor indicators of acceptance. Nor do I speak of "flight." Residential mobility, especially of homeowners, is far too complex and too tied to housing market factors to be adequately conveyed by this term. But as long as people can avoid or withdraw from systems under busing orders by one means or another, a considerable amount of public acceptance is necessary, or the gradual processes of attrition within those metropolitan areas where the masses of poor black children live will continue with at least as much intensity as they now have.

The justification usually advanced for these court actions, where so many regard the constitutional basis as doubtful, the "legislative facts" changeful, and the consequences so uncertain, is that there is no alternative. The courts *can* press this lever and produce a busing order, whereas they apparently cannot, for example, compel a distribution of educational resources on a basis of need. Nor can they compel other more powerful societal reforms of a redistributive nature. It often happens, however, that the strategy that claims "practicality" as its chief virtue turns out to be quite impractical. Our experience with busing orders may teach the courts and the rest of us more than could be learned from the best of social science testimony. But there is a considerable risk that this course of action that has so divided old allies will impair our capacity, never strong enough, to strive in other ways for a more just and humane society.

Notes

[1] A. T. Mason, The Supreme Court: temple and forum, 48 *Yale Review* 524 (1959), as quoted in Walter F. Murphy and C. Herman Pritchett, *Courts, Judges and Politics* (New York: Random House, 1961), p. 679.

[2] Alfred H. Kelly, The school desegregation case, in John A. Garraty, ed., *Quarrels That Have Shaped the Constitution* (New York: Harper & Row, 1964), p. 260.

[3] Nathaniel R. Jones, NAACP General Counsel, as quoted in *Detroit Free Press*, December 8, 1975: "Dr. James Coleman is a fraud . . . thoroughly repudiated by his colleagues. . . ."

[4] *The New York Times*, June 11, 1972, quoted Kenneth Clark as describing some studies as "a sophisticated type of backlash"; that "some social scientists were now beclouding the issues." See also his Social policy, power and social science research, *Perspectives on Inequality*, Reprint series #8, *Harvard Educational Review*, 1973, especially pp. 81, 82, and 84, for similar comments about Jencks' work, including that of showing "underlying racial biases."

[5] Eleanor P. Wolf, Civil rights and social science data, 14 *Race* 155-182 (1972).

[6] Alfred H. Kelly, Clio and the Court: an illicit love affair, in Philip B. Kurland, ed., *The Supreme Court Review* (Chicago: University of Chicago Press, 1965).

[7] Leon Friedman, ed., *The Oral Argument, Brown v. Board of Education of Topeka 1952-55* (New York: Chelsea Pub., 1969), p. 375, Mr. Nabrit.

[8] *Ibid.*, p. 402, Mr. Marshall.

[9]Owen Fiss, The jurisprudence of busing, 39 *Law and Contemporary Problems* 201 (1975).

[10]Empirical research to investigate the harmful effects of racial isolation or concentration requires comparison with racially-mixed situations. For summaries of this and similar research, see Henry M. Levin, Education, life chances, and the courts: the role of social science evidence, 39 *Law and Contemporary Problems* 217-240 (1975); Elizabeth G. Cohen, The effects of desegregation on race relations, 39 *Law and Contemporary Problems* 271-299 (1975); and Edgar G. Epps, Impact of school desegregation on aspirations, self-concepts and other aspects of personality, 39 *Law and Contemporary Problems* 300-313 (1975). The most comprehensive evaluation of such research is Nancy St. John, *Desegregation Outcomes for Children* (New York: Wiley, 1975).

[11]Paul Sheatsley, White attitudes toward the Negro, in Talcott Parsons and Kenneth Clark, eds., *The Negro American* (Boston: Little, Brown, 1966), p. 305.

[12]Jonathan Kelly, The politics of school busing, 38 *Public Opinion Quarterly* 24, 38 (1974), especially note 8. See also James A. Davis, Busing, *Southern Schools*, II, NORC Report No. 124B, University of Chicago, 1973, pp. 83-86.

[13]This was, of course, the chief and by far the most astonishing finding of James Coleman, *et al.*, *Equality of Educational Opportunity* (Washington, C.D.: U.S. Office of Education, 1966). As late as January of that year, Attorney General Katzenbach stated that "poor academic achievement in slum schools was entirely the consequence" of inadequate resources and "not the race or *economic* situation of the students" (letter of January 14, 1966). Such appraisals were widespread.

[14]Joe Feagin, ed., *The Urban Scene* (New York: Random House, 1973), pp. 182-183.

[15]*Hobson v. Hansen*, 269 F. Supp. 401 (1967) at 406, 407.

[16]*Bradley v. Milliken*, 338 F. Supp. 582 (E.D. Mich. 1971), and *Bradley v. Milliken*, 484 F. 2d 215 (Sixth Circuit 1973).

[17]See Paul Rosen, *The Supreme Court and Social Science* (Champagne: University of Illinois Press, 1972), p. 28. In *Buck v. Bell*, 274 U.S. 200 (1927), Justice Holmes's opinion upholding Virginia's compulsory sterilization law reflected the influence of yesterday's "science" (the eugenics movement): "Wholesale social regeneration . . . cannot be affected appreciably by tinkering with the institution of p׳operty but only by taking in hand life and trying to build a race."

[18]Eleanor P. Wolf, Social science and the courts: the Detroit schools case, 42 *The Public Interest* 106-108 (1976). See also William Grant, The Detroit school case: an historical overview, 21 *Wayne Law Review* 860-861 (1975), for his discussion of Judge Roth's pre-trial views.

[19]Owen Fiss, School desegregation: the uncertain path of the law, 4 *Philosophy and Public Affairs* 3-39 (1974), especially pp. 26 and 38. See also The Charlotte-Mecklenburg case—its significance for northern school desegregation, 38 *University of Chicago Law Review* 697-709 (1971).

[20]Fiss, Charlotte-Mecklenberg case, at 705.

[21]Almost one-third of the body of Judge Roth's ruling had been devoted to materials on demographic trends and residential patterns, and he had asserted an

"affirmative obligation to . . . compensate for and avoid incorporation into the school system the effects of residential social segregation"; *Bradley v. Milliken* at 593. It must be noted that the opinion of the Sixth Circuit Court of Appeals specifically rejected any dependence on residential patterns as the basis for its ruling [*Bradley v. Milliken*, 484 F. 2d (Sixth Circuit 1973) at 242], and omitted Judge Roth's reference to the "affirmative obligation" of the school authorities. For a description of the leadership in the Detroit system before the recall in 1970 that removed several Board members from office, see William Grant, The Detroit school case; also Community control vs. integration: the case of Detroit, 24 *The Public Interest* 62-79 (1971). Judge Roth devoted a number of pages in his ruling of September 1971 to praise of the system's accomplishments on behalf of integrated education.

[22]Mark Yudolf, Equal educational opportunity and the courts, 51 *Texas Law Review* 411-504 (1973).

[23]After enumerating a large number of government practices that were involved in the creation of segregated housing, Judge Roth concluded: "blacks, like ethnic groups in the past, have tended to separate from the larger group and associate together. The ghetto is at once a place of confinement and a refuge. There is enough blame for everyone to share." *Bradley v. Milliken*, 338 F. Supp. (E.D. Mich. 1971) at 592.

[24]Yudof, Equal educational opportunity, p. 457.

[25]For example, Andrew Greeley and Peter Ross, Are religious schools divisive?, in *The Education of Catholic Americans* (Chicago: Aldine, 1966) (on effects on attitudes of sectarian—and "segregated"—education); see also Levin, Education, life chances, and the courts, p. 231; Cohen, Effects of desegregation; Y. Amir, The contact hypothesis in ethnic relations, 71 *Psychological Bulletin* 319-342 (1969).

[26]Gordon Foster for NAACP (Detroit Remedy Transcript, pp. 359-369) described "racially un-identifiable schools" as those that are of uniform "racial composition," i.e., that reflect the racial make-up in the district. Such schools, he said, regardless of their proportion black, would benefit children *because* of their uniformity by improving their "self-concepts" (p. 364), by "self-fulfilling prophecy . . . expectations" (p. 364), "equal delivery of service" (p. 365), and "having a common lot with others" (p. 367).

[27]This collision is also evident in public response to remedy explanations. The discussions of cost-benefit calculations confirm citizens' beliefs that the original ruling was made on this basis; when lawyers explain to them that this was not the case, they are baffled. Thus, at a parent-teacher meeting I attended after the Supreme Court ruling on Detroit, a school board attorney explained that, if the District Court followed some precedent cases, each school might be required to approximate the overall proportion of 75% black to the extent this was feasible. When asked if this was the proportion that the "Supreme Court thinks is the best for education," he responded: "No, no, it has nothing to do with *that*."

[28]Frank T. Read, Judicial evolution of the law of school integration since *Brown v. Board of Education*, 39 *Law and Contemporary Problems* 45 (1975).

[29]Quoted by Betsy Levin and Willis D. Hawley, Foreword, 39 *Law and Contemporary Problems* 3 (1975), footnote 10.

[30] Some astute observations related to this point are made by Levin, Education, life chances, and the courts, p. 234.

[31] Jerome Frank, *Courts on Trial: Myth and Reality in American Justice* (Princeton: Princeton University Press, 1973), pp. 80-85, cited in Murphy and Pritchett, *Courts, Judges and Politics*, pp. 327-331. They note (pp. 317-319) that this "highly ritualized trial by battle of wits" is strikingly unsuitable for broad social issues.

[32] Transcript, p. 515.

[33] Transcript, pp. 1765-1766.

[34] Transcript, p. 988.

[35] Transcript, pp. 3834-3835.

[36] Transcript, p. 510.

[37] Transcript, p. 772.

[38] Nancy St. John, *Desegregation Outcomes*.

[39] Fiss, School desegregation.

[40] For an analysis of some of these problems as they affect the Supreme Court, and proposals to deal with them, see Arthur S. Miller and Jerome A. Barron, The Supreme Court, the adversary system, and the flow of information to the justices: a preliminary inquiry, 61 *Virginia Law Review* 1187 ff (1975).

[41] See Geoffrey C. Hazard, Jr., Limitations on the uses of behavioral science in the law, 19 *Case Western Reserve Law Review* 71-77 (1967), for a discussion of this problem.

[42] Frederick Mosteller and Daniel P. Moynihan, eds., *Equality of Educational Opportunity* (New York: Vintage, 1972).

[43] Detroit Remedy Hearings, 1972, pp. 520-521. (The Coleman Report had not, of course, said this in the first place. See p. 307.)

[44] James Coleman, Coleman on the Coleman Report, 1 *The Educational Researcher* 13-14 (1972).

[45] Metro Remedy Hearings, 1972, pp. 1389-1390. The expert for the Detroit Schools had no wish to weaken the impact of the Coleman material. He had earlier argued so fervently on behalf of a Metro plan that, when counsel asked what he would suggest if Detroit were completely surrounded by water, he replied: "Build a long bridge . . . no matter how large the body of water. . . ." Detroit Remedy Hearings, 1972, p. 643.

[46] Metro Remedy Hearings, 1972, p. 1389.

[47] Metro Remedy Hearings, 1972, pp. 977-979.

[48] My version, not a quotation.

[49] Yudof, Equal educational opportunity, p. 439.

[50] Deposition of David Armor, May 24, 1972, Cambridge, Mass. V.X., Joint Appendix, U.S. Court of Appeals, No. 72-8002, pp. xa262–xa393.

[51] Findings of Fact and Conclusions of Law in Support of Ruling on Desegregation Area and Development of Plan, E.D. Mich., June 14, 1972. C.A. 35257. The citation was to *Monroe v. Board of Commissioners, Jackson, Tenn.*, 427 2d 1005, 1008 (C.A. 6, 1970).

[52] There is a continuous flow of articles in the law journals, the main theme of which appears to be a search for an intellectually satisfying legal basis for declaring

northern school segregation unconstitutional. The intensity of this quest suggests to the layman that the basis is so elusive and ambiguous that the development of public understanding and support for such decisions will continue to be difficult. For a comprehensive and penetrating review of alternative grounds for judicial action in the northern school cases, see Frank Goodman, *De facto* school segregation: a constitutional and empirical analysis, 60 *California Law Review* 275-437 (1972).

Index